D0903681

ARISTOTLE

PHILOSOPHERS · IN · CONTEXT

ARISTOTLE

J.D.G. Evans

Professor of Logic and Metaphysics,
Queen's University, Belfast

THE HARVESTER PRESS · SUSSEX

ST. MARTIN'S PRESS · NEW YORK

First published in Great Britain in 1987 by
THE HARVESTER PRESS LIMITED
Publisher: John Spiers
16 Ship Street, Brighton, Sussex
and in the USA by
ST. MARTIN'S PRESS, INC.
175 Fifth Avenue, New York, NY 10010

British Library Cataloguing in Publication Data
Evans, J.D.G.
Aristotle — (Philosophers in context)
1. Aristotle
I. Title II. Series
185 B485

ISBN 0–7108–1042–3

Library of Congress Cataloging-in-Publication Data
Evans, J.D.G. (John David Gemmill), 1942–
Aristotle.

Bibliography: p.
Includes index.
1. Aristotle. I. Title.
B485.E93 1987 185 86–27964
ISBN 0-312-00485-0

Typeset in 11pt Times by Woodfield Graphics, Fontwell,
Arundel, West Sussex

Printed and bound in Great Britain by
Biddles Ltd, Guildford and King's Lynn

To Romi

Contents

Preface

The work of any philosopher needs to be assessed in two kinds of context. The first is the context provided by his own intellectual environment. What does the philosopher owe to those whose work he read, was influenced by and reacted against? Aristotle is committed by his own dialectical method to basing his discussions on the views and problems which were generated by his environment. The theoretical rationale for this method is examined in Chapter 1, and in subsequent chapters it will become clear how Aristotle gives practical execution to this theory as he confronts major philosophical problems.

The second kind of context is the present state of philosophy. Where does the philosopher stand when judged by developments in the subject since his time? Aristotle's treatment of many issues can be properly appreciated only by comparing it with those of subsequent philosophers; and this is done at a number of points in this book. Aristotle is the figure in the history of philosophy who, more than any other, claims the attention and allegiance of all who work in any of the many styles and traditions of philosophy. Indeed he may be the only philosopher of whom this can be said. So both these kinds of context provide an entirely suitable means of approaching Aristotle's philosophy with the aim of obtaining a general grasp of its nature.

The project of this book is to provide a thorough analysis of the nature and purpose of Aristotle's philosophy as a whole. Not every aspect of his work is treated; for example, I say virtually nothing about his exercises in logical and aesthetic theory. But I have addressed the main and pervasive themes of his philosophising, and in the course of examining these I try to distil the characteristic style of his thought.

There are other books, some of them recently written, which offer a comprehensive treatment of Aristotle, and I have derived much from their scholarly accuracy and philosophical acumen. But in my view none of them altogether succeeds in providing a convincing or a correct diagnosis of the motivation in Aristotle's selection and treatment of his topics. A principal aim of my own study is to emphasise the *dialectical* character of his philosophical style. The importance of dialectic in both the theory and the practice of Aristotle's method has been recognised by others; but here I apply this insight, more systematically and in greater detail than others have done, to a wide range of centrally important Aristotelian discussions.

I am conscious of many influences that have gone into the conception and execution of this book. Foremost among these have been the comments and reactions of generations of students at Cambridge, Duke and Belfast; the need to excite and retain their attention has been a potent spur towards the discovery of a philosophically satisfying reading of Aristotle. Earlier versions of some sections were read to groups at Belfast and Ballymascanlon; and Max Wright, Jonathan Gorman and Jack Copeland were among those who made helpful comments. Christopher McKnight read the whole draft and made some invaluable suggestions, as did Stephan Körner and Christopher Rowe.

The typing of the final draft was an immense labour which was executed with efficiency and unfailing cheerfulness by Lindsay Osborne and Mary Emmerson. But the greatest contribution came from my wife, who removed many infelicities of style and presentation. The book could not have been written without her encouragement and support.

Abbreviations and References to the Works of Aristotle

Titles of Aristotle's works are abbreviated as follows:

Cat.	*Categories*
De Int.	*De Interpretatione*
An. Pr.	*Prior Analytics*
An. Post.	*Posterior Analytics*
Top.	*Topics*
S.E.	*De Sophisticis Elenchis*
Phys.	*Physics*
Cael.	*De Caelo*
G.C.	*De Generatione et Corruptione*
Mete.	*Meteorologica*
De An.	*De Anima*
P.A.	*De Partibus Animalium*
M.A.	*De Motu Animalium*
G.A.	*De Generatione Animalium*
Met.	*Metaphysics*
E.N.	*Nicomachean Ethics*
E.E.	*Eudemian Ethics*
Pol.	*Politics*
Rhet.	*Rhetoric*

All references to the works of Aristotle are by the standard system defined by the title of work, book, chapter, page, column and line in the edition of I. Bekker (Berlin, 1831). Thus *Met.* Z14, 1039b2-6, refers to lines 2 to 6 of the right-hand column of page 1039, which occurs in chapter 14 of book Z (in fact, the seventh book) of the *Metaphysics*.

I have used the texts of the Oxford Classical Texts series where these are available, and in other cases (*Mete.*, *P.A.*, *M.A.*, *E.E.*) the Loeb series. Any departures from these texts are noted.

All translations are my own; but I gratefully acknowledge the help afforded by earlier versions, especially those in the excellent Clarendon Aristotle Series under the editorship of J.L. Ackrill.

CHAPTER 1

The Intellectual Background

Aristotle is the philosopher's philosopher. His writing has shaped philosophical concerns, and has directed the interest of philosophers, to an extent unmatched by any other. The fashions of philosophical orthodoxy may shift, dislodging different thinkers from pre-eminence at different times, but Aristotle's place on everybody's select list is constant.

The purpose of this whole book is to explain why Aristotle occupies this key position in philosophy. Let us approach his philosophical enterprise by examining his intellectual background. With any thinker it is important to understand the issues of contemporary concern which provided the motivation for his pronouncements. They may not be the same as those which appear most relevant to us today, and so some historical detail will be needed if we are to secure a proper intellectual perspective. With Aristotle this point of method cuts much deeper than in the general case. As we have said, his thought is set firmly in the intellectual problems of his time; and, furthermore, it is essential to his conception of philosophy that he should fully reflect and respond to the influences of his background.

Aristotle finds the motive and direction for his whole enterprise in an inheritance of problems and conflicts of view among his predecessors and contemporaries. He says, 'What seems to everyone to be the case, we declare to be true.'[1] Where there is no disagreement, there is nothing for him to work on. Conversely, where there really is a problem, its terms are set by the nature of the disagreement in the views that other people take.

Aristotle and Philosophy

Philosophy thrives on controversy. Many philosophers would agree that this is true, but few would follow Aristotle in seeing this as the basis of the essential nature of philosophical investigation. Some have believed that it is its distinctive field of topics and problems that marks philosophy off from other subjects. For example, there is the trio of concepts which Kant took to be the subject matter of traditional metaphysics—God, freedom and immortality.[2] Kant's own discussion of these topics has greatly assisted the rejection of this conception of the philosopher's function; but even so, we may reflect on how easy it would be today—say, with reference to the teaching and research activities of a university philosophy department—to give a topic-based description.

Still, most contemporary philosophers would subscribe to a rather different account of what they are about. They believe that philosophy is distinguished from other enquiries not by its subject matter but by its methods and focus of interest. Typically philosophers are interested in the concepts employed in making certain claims; they examine our right to feel that we have a clear grasp of the nature of these concepts. The substantive truth or falsity of the claims involved is a matter for other, less abstract disciplines.[3]

In Aristotle there is no trace of this view of philosophy. Indeed he provides the materials for its refutation. Nor is he at all inclined to accept the alternative view that philosophy has a special and esoteric subject matter. Consider, for example, the analysis of the way we should live. Should the philosophical approach give us an ideal blueprint for life even though this contains a virtually superhuman prescription? Some have supposed so. Others maintain that the principal task is to analyse the judgements which can be made about directives to live in some particular way.[4] Aristotle is concerned simply with the question of how we are to become and remain good people—a question, he believes, that calls for the full resources of our rational and practical powers, given that rational and practical agents are what we are.

The same pattern is apparent in his work in psychology and ontology. In neither of these fields does he confine his attention to some specifically metaphysical aspect of the subject, such as the immortality of the soul or the existence of abstract objects; nor is he occupied with purely conceptual problems rather than substantive issues of fact. He is interested in the nature of thought but also in the nature of hearing; and when he discusses hearing, he also explores the physical basis of sound. His ontological theory embraces both the exotic and controversial—God, numbers, universals—and the humdrum and familiar existence of physical objects; and about the latter he asks simply what they really are.

Aristotle is indeed much concerned with the distinctions and overlaps between different kinds of study. But in his complicated chartings of the territory of human knowledge philosophy as such does not appear.[5] So can our initial claim that Aristotle is the very paradigm of philosophy be sustained? We shall find that it can be, and in the process we shall discover something important about the nature of philosophy itself.

Every significant problem to which Aristotle addresses himself is prefaced by an examination of what his contemporaries had to say about it. This is as true of large problems occupying the whole works, such as the nature of change or of the soul, as it is of problems of smaller compass, such as the nature of friendship. We shall see how this method actually works in later chapters. Here we shall consider what it promises to deliver. Consider this passage from the preface to the discussion of friendship in the *Eudemian Ethics*:

> We must accept the reasoning which will both best exhibit for us the views held about these matters and at the same time resolve the difficulties and conflicts; and we will achieve this if we show that the conflicting views are held with good reason. For such reasoning will most closely accord with the agreed facts; and it will allow the conflicting views to be retained if each is partly true and partly false. (H2, 1235b13-18)

This is a particularly clear and characteristic statement of how Aristotle thinks a philosophical discussion should start and how it should then move on.

There is in this passage a twofold theme, the need for conservation and the need for development. We must start from the available views, stick to agreed facts, and try to reach an end-result where the original conflict of views is in some way retained. At the same time, the conflict will be resolved by a sifting process which separates elements of truth and falsity from the different views. Thus refined, the views can then be combined and reconciled in a way that was not possible before the critical analysis. The conflicting views remain, but only in the sense that the conflict has been eliminated from them. The whole process starts from juxtaposing different views which, it seems, cannot coherently be combined; the task of analysis is to show that this appearance is wrong, since on the best understanding of the contributions to truth contained in the views, they should be regarded as complementing each other.

The parties to the debate see themselves in conflict, so that if one is right, the others are wrong; and they are right in this—that each and every view, as construed by the conflicting parties, is wrong. But they are all wrong in failing to see the possibility of reconciliation which Aristotle's analysis will reveal. It is no accident if this appears to anticipate the idea of dialectic as developed in Kantian and post-Kantian philosophy. Aristotelian dialectic is a precursor of the later method, although Aristotle himself would certainly regard its full development as a perversion of his insights. We must now look more closely at the philosophical merits of Aristotle's own analysis.

An extensive illustration of how Aristotle sets about rehearsing discrepant views to sift true from false comes in *Metaphysics* B, where the discussion of fourteen problems occupies a whole book.[6] The first chapter is a preface to the exercise and has some important comments on the purpose and justification of the method. Aristotle starts with a thought which will have seemed fresher to him than it may to us, familiar as we are with the image of being tied up in knots by dilemmas. He compares those who are caught in a problem to those who are tied up; for both, freedom can come only by untying the knot. They must realise this as a precondition for their release.[7]

So far we have a recommended strategy for freedom from intellectual difficulty which depends on recognising the problems in which one is ensnared. But this will only be convincing to those who accept the simile of physical bondage; and why should we construe our mental state in this way? Aristotle invokes here an old problem from Plato's *Meno.* How can a person seeking a solution to some intellectual problem find the way forward, given that it is his ignorance of the way forward that precisely defines the problem?[8] Plato does well to pose the problem; but his solution to it—that the answer is really in our minds all along, and only needs to be excited to the surface of consciousness—amounts to no more than a statement of faith that the problem can be solved. Aristotle shows how we can make better sense of Plato's problem, and devise a more convincing strategy for resolving it, if we realise that what sets the stage is a conflict of available views.

In the presence of such a conflict we cannot make progress because the accounts on offer seem to cancel each other out. That the views disagree is clear; what we need to understand is why they disagree. Only then will we have some sense of the way forward. The leading idea is that in order to identify the problem and to avoid a route which will merely take us back into it, we must pay attention to the conflict of views.

So we see that the examination of current and previous views is no mere literary or expository device for Aristotle but something that is utterly integral to philosophical progress. Here we have the materials for a distinctively Aristotelian conception of philosophy, one that deserves to take its place beside the two conceptions mentioned earlier. Aristotle has a theory, expounded chiefly in the *Posterior Analytics*, of how a fully developed body of scientific understanding should look. It is based on the foundations of indubitable axioms, from which the remaining truths of the science are derived as theorems by a strict and necessary process of deductive proof. Not everything in a science can be proved; but what cannot be proved—the foundations—can be directly and immediately known.[9] This model is mainly illustrated by the mathematical sciences; but Aristotle also has it in mind throughout his investigations into nature and change.[10]

A central thesis of this theory of science is that the dividing-lines between different specialisms should be recognised and respected. For it is scarcely plausible that every truth should be derivable from the same axiomatic base. Aristotle fits into this scheme the various mathematical and natural sciences, as well as his study of existence, and the practical and productive skills, such as ethics and rhetoric. But there is a further and very important element in his account of scientific understanding: the role played by dialectic.[11] The theory of science as an axiomatised deductive structure concerns the presentation of established bodies of knowledge rather than the processes of discovery that take us to such knowledge. Such discovery is a messier business, and is not susceptible to the neat regimentation imposed by the theory of science. In dialectic we avail ourselves of a vast range of considerations and techniques, including particularly the prevailing views, both expert and lay, and the deliverances of common sense as evidenced in ordinary habits of thought and talk. When Aristotle justifies some claim by appeal to what 'we say', this is a device of intellectual discovery which is sanctioned by his theory of dialectic.

Dialectic provides a method for approaching every kind of topic. Here we abandon the emphasis on specialisation that is so prominent in the theory of science; on the contrary, a leading aspect of dialectic is the way in which it uses concepts and procedures that cross the boundaries of disciplines. Aristotle's concept of dialectic is something that he develops by reflection on a tradition of question-and-answer debate which was already at least a century old in his time. The Greeks who engaged in this debate had an intuitive sense of its value in providing a disciplined context for teasing out philosophical problems; and Aristotle's attempt to justify assigning this method a key place in enquiry is an endorsement of their intuition.[12]

No philosopher's actual procedure is likely to accord perfectly with his official methodology. All descriptions of method involve a considerable degree of idealisation, even if they are essentially accurate—which they often are not. Aristotle is a selfconscious philosopher, and his method in an investigation follows his theoretical methodology unusually closely; but the match is not perfect. From the foregoing description of his theory of method one might expect his actual discussion of some particular subject matter to consist of two phases. First, there would be a dialectical application of general considerations and a review of prevailing opinions, with the aim of reaching the fundamental axioms for the particular discipline. The second phase would be the strictly scientific operation of deducing the special theorems of the science from these axioms. All these elements are in fact present in Aristotle's actual investigations; but they are run much more closely together than the methodology would suggest, so that the theoretical separation into two phases is misleading. A typical investigation exhibits a thorough intermingling of all the elements listed.

So here we have the distinctively Aristotelian approach to philosophy. Philosophy is not concerned with a special subject matter; such specialisation is what marks a science off from philosophy. But neither does philosophy incorporate a different kind of focus on the topics of each science. In this sense philosophy is continuous with science, in much the way that Quine maintains through his holistic conception of knowledge.[13] But this is not to reduce philosophy to science, and what underpins its autonomy is the ineliminable presence of the dialectical elements in Aristotle's style of handling particular problems. Chief among these dialectical features is the unravelling of those conflicts set up by the combination of prevailing views.

We come back to the importance of this most prominent aspect of his philosophical work. We have examined the justification in theory for his practice. His advice to philosophers can be put very simply. Start from where you are, and unravel and elucidate the problems in which your thinking is caught; this is the only way to make real progress of the reflective sort which is philosophy's style. The best philosophers have shown in practice their instinct for this method; but none, I think, has so effectively articulated its rationale as Aristotle.

So we should now examine the leading features of the philosophical environment in which Aristotle worked. The major figures are the Presocratics—the succession of thinkers from Thales to Democritus—and Plato; and by far the most important of these is Plato. Aristotle studied and worked in Plato's Academy for nearly twenty years. But to know that is to risk being misled into believing that their intellectual relationship was more intimate that it seems to have been. A careful study of the way in which Aristotle actually discusses Plato's views reveals that his treatment of Plato's ideas proceeds entirely by way of the latter's written works—that is, works which are equally available to us.[14] This is also true of the writing of the Presocratics, except that we possess their works only in a much more excerpted form than Aristotle evidently did: indeed the form and extent of our knowledge of these excerpts is largely Aristotle's own doing.

So the inheritance of views on which his work is based, is equally available for us to inspect and evaluate.

Let us consider in turn three elements in this inheritance which Aristotle finds of pervasive importance in his philosophical work: the nature of reality, the problem of change, and the principles by which the study of things should be organised. It should be understood that my aim in the following sections is to highlight what Aristotle took to be the main features of his predecessors' ideas on these topics. Many objections could be raised—and have been—as to the adequacy of Aristotle's focus and the correctness of his interpretations; and Aristotle himself has much more to say on the philosophical issues raised here, as we shall see in later chapters of this book. Here my interest is in setting the agenda for the later discussions.

The Nature of Reality

The Greeks had no particularly exotic ideas about existence. The centre of focus is at all times on perceptible objects of medium size in the vicinity of the theorist. But speculation on what it is that confers reality on such objects led the early thinkers down tracks that ended in paradox. We encounter such claims as that everything is water, or there is only one thing, or that numbers are substances. Aristotle, ever the defender of common sense against paradox, compared such pronouncements to the ravings of madmen, except that they are both more and less absurd than such ravings: more, because no one is so mad as to maintain such things, but also less, because they are maintained on a basis of reasoning.[15] Even so, such accounts still represent attempts to arrive at the true nature of familiar physical objects. God and the human soul are also subjects of ontological speculation; and here again, since the prevailing climate of opinion was not agnostic, ontology was following the broad indications of ordinary thought.

But there is a major exception to this generally sober trend in ontology, and that is Plato's theory of Forms. Plato maintains that certain objects, which are definitely not present to familiar and ordinary experience, nonetheless really exist.[16] He argues that familiar experience presupposes the existence of Forms, but he denies that they are actually encountered by the intellect which remains unstimulated by philosophy. Aristotle thinks the theory deeply wrong—flawed in its overall conception and open to a host of detailed objections within its own terms. It is sometimes supposed, wrongly, that Aristotle simply amended Plato's theory in certain details, substituting for a theory of transcendent universals a view of universals as immanent. On the contrary, he rejected the claim that there are such objects as Forms and regarded Plato's theory as a misconceived account of something that does exist, namely form.

Plato's theory of Forms states that in addition to the physical, perceptible objects with which we are all familiar, there are extra objects which are non-physical and imperceptible; and it is by virtue of these properties that the latter objects (the Forms) are more real than the former. We can specify the contents of this realm of reality more precisely: wherever we have a unit of intelligibility—such as the meaning of a single word—we have one Platonic Form. Thus, although we are familiar in the world of sense experience with many things that are large or beautiful, the use of a single univocal word to characterise each of the members of these pluralities points to an awareness of a single object separate from and yet reflected in the plurality. This single object is the Form. It is what the words 'large' and 'beautiful' primarily refer to; only by an extension of meaning, which reduces the sharpness of our understanding, can these words also refer to the objects we encounter in sense experience.[17]

Aristotle is an unrelenting opponent of the ontological extravagance of the theory of Forms. Some of his prominent objections are adapted from difficulties which Plato himself indicates in his *Parmenides*; this demonstrates, incidentally, that Aristotle saw that work as a repository of genuine and serious flaws in the theory of Forms. He presses the objection known as the Third Man.[18] This argument exploits a feature of the language in which the theory of Forms is presented: Forms are characteristically introduced by *predicates*, such as 'large' and 'beautiful', but according to the theory these are names of *objects*. The theory seems to embody a confusion between things and the properties of things or, in terms of semantics, between what names refer to and what predicates designate.

This difficulty is part of a larger problem that Aristotle

discovers when he tries to compare Forms and physical objects: the theory systematically obliterates the differences between things which any proper theory of categories should require us to respect. Consider, for example, properties which relate things. Certain things are similar; that is, they are similar to something. Certain things are large; this means that they are large in relation to something. So in calling things 'similar' or 'large', or in thinking of them in these terms, we speak and think elliptically, since there must be at least implicit reference to some further thing.[19] This abbreviated way of treating such relative properties is, of course, typically harmless. But there is a danger here, and Plato is not alert to it. We must avoid a theory about these properties which will cause us to treat them in an absolute, non-relative way.[20]

Compare 'Socrates is large' and 'Socrates is similar'. If we are inclined to construe 'large' in the first sentence as referring to an object which is only loosely connected with Socrates, we may be inclined also to construe 'similar' in this manner in the second sentence. Aristotle argues that the two analyses *should* go together; so Plato's approach must be wrong. Both analyses are to be rejected, and the patent absurdity of the second shows the only slightly less obvious unacceptability of the first.

To construe 'similar' on the model of 'large' is to fail to recognise the difference between a two-place and a one-place predicate. This is a clear case of a category mistake. But to suppose that any predicate, whether one-place or many-place, can refer to an object, is to make the same kind of mistake. Aristotle is aware that Plato says things about the predicate 'large' that raise doubts about whether it is in fact one-place.[21] But this is just his point: Plato's handling of predicates is bound to undermine any attempt to make distinctions between their different kinds. So much the worse, then, for the whole approach to predicates. It is likely to fail precisely because it misconstrues all predicates as names of objects.

The bearing of category distinctions on the nature of objects and their properties will be examined in Chapter 3. But one difficulty needs to be considered here. Certain properties serve quite generally to distinguish Forms from physical objects. Examples are immutability and intelligibility by pure reason; every Form has these properties, and any physical object is excluded from possessing them. So the properties are of categorial status in Plato's theory since they serve to divide objects at the most basic ontological level.[22] But now comes the difficulty. Does it make sense to maintain, in the case of some particular kind of thing (such as a man or a red thing) that in addition to those that undergo change and are perceptible to the senses there exists a further specimen of which these properties do not hold? Immobile men and invisible red objects sound self-contradictory.[23] The main point is that a theory of categories should provide a scheme which reflects obvious divisions between things and does not divide up what should be grouped together. Thus the integrity of such groupings as men and red things should certainly be preserved, even though we may discover a fundamental distinction *between* these two groups. Plato's theory of Forms suffers fatally when it is judged as, and by the standards of, a theory of categories.

Sometimes Aristotle puts his objection even more simply. Plato's ontology is deeply motivated by the desire to explain the objects which we encounter, in their amorphous pluralities, in ordinary experience. The Forms impose order on this mass of experience and thereby promise to make it intelligible. In response to this strategy Aristotle has a simple and fundamental objection. How can it be sound, if we have difficulty in making sense of some plurality of objects, to resolve the obscurity by adding to the objects to be considered? We may call this the *counting problem*. If your difficulty arises because there are, say, a thousand objects to explain, you do not make progress by adding to this number of objects; a thousand-and-one objects are no easier to explain than a thousand.[24]

Would Plato find this Aristotelian objection captious? He might say that it ignores the special status of his one thousand-and-first object which, like an original work of art, could clarify the obscurities of a thousand copies.[25] Such a reply would miss Aristotle's point. The counting problem highlights the extravagance of introducing obscure and paradoxical entities in order to resolve difficulties in our understanding of things which, however obscure, unquestionably do exist. Aristotle's whole opposition to Plato's ontology may be summed up thus: any adequate solution to problems raised by things which exist, must be resolved by attending to those very things. To bring further objects into the picture is liable to stir up a host of detailed ontological difficulties of the kinds we have considered, and is ultimately fruitless.

Aristotle is rather less concerned with the ontological speculations of the Presocratics, which is a measure of the importance he attaches to Plato's contribution. But the Presocratics have one very important contribution to make to the debate, and that is their emphasis on speculating about the constituents from which things are made. They thus embark on the search for the nature of matter, but haltingly and uncertainly, just as Plato is unsure in his pursuit of form.

For the most part, the Presocratics were concerned to simplify the ontological contents of the world, not to add to them. Thus they tended to say that despite the apparent diversity of things that confront the uninstructed mind, the underlying reality is much simpler and more uniform. They approached their work in this way partly from a desire to provide for the possibility of explaining change. Radical changes, such as the transformation of one substance into another, will seem less mysterious if we can show that the true substance, underlying the appearances, is not altered in the change; substantial change will be reduced to the more tractable phenomenon of change of quality.[26] We shall consider this response in more detail shortly. Another motive is the perennial scientific desire for simplicity. An explanation is superior if it invokes fewer factors to account for more; and the ultimate goal of this ideal of explanation is to explain everything in terms of one single thing.[27]

Aristotle portrays the Presocratics as struggling towards his conception of matter. It is important to understand why he thought that they largely failed in that struggle. The basic defect in their conception was a neglect of that aspect of things that Plato emphasises so much—their form.[28] The world as we encounter it has structure and organisation. It is of the nature of matter as such that it should lack structure. Therefore any attempt to construe matter in accordance with the items of familiar experience must be wrong.

So when Thales says that all things are water, he cannot be providing a satisfactory account of the matter of all things, since water is one of the structured and organised substances that we encounter in the world. Some of the Presocratics may have evinced a sense of this difficulty by suggesting that the material substrate was not precisely identical with the corresponding substance which presents itself to ordinary experience. In semantic terms (although putting the point in this way is anachronistic for the Presocratics) 'water' is ambiguous as it is applied now to the familiar stuff which we drink and wash in and now to the ultimate substance of all things.[29]

The Problem of Change

Aristotle's own speculations on existence are shaped by the interests of, and what he believed to be the shortcomings in these predecessors. Reflection on their work helped to produce his most central ideas on the nature of matter and form and on the significance of category distinctions. The problem of change is a second leading theme which provides a fundamental link between Aristotle's philosophy and earlier theorising. His general complaint is that no earlier thinker adequately grasped the deep importance of this feature of the reality they sought to explain.

How fair is this as a charge against Plato? It might seem that it is not fair at all. For his two-world ontology establishes liability to change and stability as a main basis of the distinction between the realm of physical objects and the Forms. So it seems that Plato gives full recognition to mutability as a fact about the physical; yet this is just the omission and distortion for which Aristotle berates him. Aristotle finds this reply inadequate: Plato's commitment to this ontology requires him to discount the importance of change in the physical—for the reason, above all, that this realm depends on and is explained by reference to the Forms. To seek to explain the mutable in terms of what is immutable, is to underestimate the significance of change in what is to be explained.

The difficulty is twofold. First, change is liable to be intermittent, occurring only at certain times. Yet the Forms that the theory maintains to be the causes of the physical are invariant in their relation to the things that depend on them. So it is impossible that such unchanging objects, functioning as causes for other objects, should both be invariant in their causality (as they must be) and yet produce effects which vary over time.[30]

This is a real problem; but perhaps it indicates that the view of Forms as causes is not so much wrong as incomplete. In Aristotle's own theory of causation, forms are causes in only one of the many senses of that term. The variation in the operation of such causal factors might be due to some further causal feature of a type ignored by Plato.

There is a second difficulty which cannot be answered so easily; and when we see this, we also see that the answer to the first difficulty is inadequate. For the problem now is that even as invariant causes of the permanent nature of mutable physical things, Forms are not at all matched to the task. Aristotle can best illustrate this point from the case of biology. With biological entities, the main aim is to try to understand the processes through which they originate and develop, and those further processes which constitute the execution of their particular life functions.[31] Locomotion, for example, may proceed by the movement of legs and arms over land or by the flapping of wings or fins in air or water. Both are wholly natural and efficient means for the forward propulsion of a body; but, of course, they are natural and efficient only relative to the biology of the species in question. In the same way, reproduction depends on biological constitution, and so it will occur in a quite different manner in animals and with plants; a single account of the process could not reflect this complexity.

Is Plato committed to denying these obvious facts? On the face of it, no. For reference to such differentiating features as means of locomotion and reproduction can be incorporated into the definition of each species; and the definition, according to Plato's theory, should give us an account of the unvarying conditions for membership of the species. But this is only a verbal solution. An investigator whose research strategy confines his attention to what is invariant cannot experience, and therefore cannot understand, processes of change.[32]

Aristotle draws a parallel with a project for studying optics or acoustics which excludes all reference to sensory phenomena. Such a project might be based on general scientific principles for handling what is intelligible in the world; but that precisely shows that these principles exclude the very possibility of the particular scientific enterprise. Conversely, Aristotle uses the sure fact of the viability of optics and acoustics, to cast general doubt on the view of science which would rule out these enterprises.

The difficult with biology is the same. Processes are by their very nature inaccessible as objects of study for the Platonist who confines his attention to a realm of reality where change is wholly absent.[33]

The Presocratics' study of nature was not hampered by this difficulty. They had no official theory that ruled against the intelligibility of change. Even so they were blinkered in their attempts to understand change, and conceptual inadequacies caused problems for them too as they attempted to study the natural world.

As we have seen, one of the main motives in the Presocratics' search for an ultimate substance was a desire to account for radical changes. If change of substance could be shown really to involve no more alteration than does variation in quality, then there ceases to be any special problem about radical change; for it turns out that all changes are non-radical.[34] Aristotle thinks that this assimilation between the different types of change is mistaken, and that such a mistake is an obstacle to the proper understanding of any change, whether radical or non-radical.

The problem of change is this. A change must involve the replacement of one state of affairs by another, but not any such replacement will qualify as a change. If you are looking at this book one moment and a moment later see a plate of curry where the book was, we would describe this as a case in which a book was replaced by curry but not one in which a book changed into curry. For the latter claim to be made out, we would have to detect some mechanism in the book which would enable *it* to become the curry; if we have no idea what sort of mechanism this could be, we will not accept that there is any thing which has changed, even though there has been a change in the total situation. But how could there be such a change overall and yet no change in any of the elements that make up the situation?

Aristotle's view is that for there to be any change, even radical change, there must be stability. But equally, even the least radical change, such as change of colour or complexion, will require a change *in* the subject that undergoes it. What the Presocratics underestimated or even ignored is the significance of the second requirement as against the first.[35] We need to develop an adequate conception of the subject of change: the subject possesses a propensity for change—what Aristotle calls its potentiality—and also retains a continuing identity as it survives change.

The model of change most favoured by the Presocratics was the rearrangement of basic elements into different shapes and patterns. A prominent illustration of this is the atomic theory propounded by Leucippus and Democritus, which construed every change by reference to the shapes and positions of the constituent minimal parts (atoms) of things. The general model was adopted in essentials by most of the Presocratics. This is the kind of change in which the enduring continuity of the subject is most obvious; the change within the subject is so played down that it hardly appears. The change seems to characterise not so much the subject itself as the regions of space which it enters and leaves. So if Aristotle wants to insist that a proper conception of change must locate the change firmly in the subject that undergoes it, the model of a shifting mosaic pattern will be rejected as inappropriate.

Although the Presocratics, unlike Plato, did not have a conception of reality that was professedly antithetical to change, they too were unable to give an adequate account of it. Aristotle will improve on these attempts by developing his own account of matter and exploring its relation to form, as we shall see in Chapter 5. Here we have been examining how Aristotle's problems and themes spring directly from his reflections on earlier theorising on the nature of change.

The Division of Study

The intellectual background to Aristotle's thought provides another very important factor which pervades all his work. The ideas to be examined here bear on his discussion of the articulation and organisation of study and knowledge. As we saw earlier, Aristotle is very emphatic about the need to respect the lines of division between different specialisms. This is partly because of his particular ideas about the nature of reality and of our cognitive relation to it, and partly because of his intuitive sense of the difference between effective argument and idle sophistry. Both these elements in his thinking should be seen as a commentary on earlier methods of investigation.

On the theoretical side the main impetus again comes from Plato's work. Plato saw, as no one had before, the usefulness of articulating skills and sciences into different kinds.[36] He uses these maps of knowledge to investigate the pretensions to valid status of such doubtful candidates as rhetoric; and he also draws lessons about how we should pursue such unquestionably viable sciences as arithmetic and geometry. But still for Plato the specialist conception of study is a second-best approach; indeed, he believes it to involve a distortion of the very subject matter which he is trying to understand. The supreme, ideal science is what he calls dialectic—a comprehensive and synoptic investigation into the whole of reality in all its connectedness.[37] Plato, one could say, is impressed by the idea that really to know anything, you must know everything; for is not each thing systematically related to each other thing?

Plato's striving after a unified account of all there is does no more than make explicit what is implicit in thought of the Presocratics; namely that true understanding of the complex and various is attained when we can show it to be simple and uniform. Aristotle protests that this strategy must oversimplify and misrepresent the irreducible complexities in things. Some skills relate to doing and making things; and these are to be distinguished from those skills which aim at the inactive contemplation of truth. Aristotle argues that Plato's conception of moral goodness is vitiated by this confusion of practical and theoretical truth. Even within the range of purely theoretical studies, real distinctions in subject matter must be observed if sophistical argument is not to result.

The main reason for respecting these distinctions is that things do not all fall within any one definite kind. There is no kind of thing such that every thing is of that kind.[38] Aristotle thinks that even to spell out these very immediate consequences of a holistic ontology is enough to make it implausible. But if more detail is required, ontology can very easily supply a defence of the view that things fall under irreducibly distinct kinds. This is a principal theme of Aristotle's theory of categories—his account of what it means to use general terms to characterise things. On this theory no single account is possible: general terms have a variety of roles in meaning, and there will be obfuscation if anyone tries to eliminate this variety in favour of uniformity. For example, activities are fundamentally different from states. So someone might construe the statement that a person is dreaming on the model of the statement that he is asleep; he will then mistakenly suppose that because the latter state obtains completely at an instant of time, so also must the former. Armed with his theory of categories, Aristotle objects that dreaming is not a state at all but an activity, which is completely different; so to understand the statements in such a way that both are assimilated is to fail to distinguish between distinct kinds of things.

The Platonic ideal is to provide a systematic and unified explanation of everything. It is based on the thesis that everything is related to everything else. Once we see the ambiguity in the word 'everything', the programme founders. It becomes clear that further divisions between the subjects of study need to be drawn. Numbers and shapes are both quantities; and so as far as the argument from the categories goes, they might both fall within the same science. But if we are able to resist the attraction of the synoptic ideal in its most comprehensive form, Aristotle thinks that we can go on to acknowledge finer distinctions. Scientists who run with the grain of reality will discover these. Then we will see that the deep differences between numbers and shapes should preclude any attempt to investigate both within the same intellectual enterprise.

These are admittedly rather schematic considerations. Moreover, while Aristotle's basic insight into the dangers of oversimplification is valuable, it might be felt that he exaggerates it. Post-Renaissance science, in particular, represents something of a return to Plato's ideal of a unified conception of, at least, the subject matter of mathematics and physics.

So we should note that Aristotle reveals a more informal sense—one that perhaps carries more conviction—of the unsatisfactory argument that is likely to result if the differences between various types of study are not fully recognised. Suppose that we wish to argue against the advisability of taking exercise after eating—surely a medical matter. How should we support a claim that this ought not to be attempted? One way might be to rehearse arguments—such as those of Zeno the Eleatic—that any movement is impossible, since it requires the traverse of an infinite distance. Whatever the force of such an argument, it is based wholly on considerations that belong to physics or geometry and have nothing to do with medicine. Yet the issue to which the argument is addressed is a medical one. So Zeno's argument should not be allowed in this context, even if it establishes its professed conclusion impeccably. It cannot advance our understanding of a medical problem since it makes no use of peculiarly medical considerations.[39]

Here is a more interesting example of the same point. In his work on animal reproduction Aristotle examines the phenomenon of sterility in mules. He considers the following attempt to explain why the mating of a male and female mule is unproductive. A mule is the offspring of interbreeding between a horse and an ass. This is an instance of the general genetic principle that the offspring of interbreeding is different in species from each of its parents. Corresponding to this general principle is another one: when two members of the same species breed, the offspring will be of the same species. In that case a pair of mules must be infertile. For if they mate, the offspring—if there is any—must be a mule; and yet we know that a mule is the offspring of a horse and an ass. Therefore, such a mating can produce neither a mule nor any other kind of creature; it must be sterile.[40]

Although this argument seems far more appropriate to the problem of sterility than does Zeno's to the desirability of taking exercise, it still suffers from something of the same fault. It is, one might say, too abstract in the considerations it appeals to. It has more to do with exploring the relations of similarity and dissimilarity among causal factors and their effects, than with the analysis of any specific feature of the genetics of reproduction. We object that although this argument does indeed rely on genetic principles, a formally parallel argument could be constructed on a quite unrelated topic, where all mention of genetic considerations has been eliminated.

Aristotle contrasts this argument with one based on theory about the particular substances that are causally operative in reproduction, the semen and menses. An argument based on insights into the causal properties of these substances would focus on the kinds of facts that distinguish the study of animal reproduction from all other fields of enquiry.[41]

Aristotle faults Presocratic speculation for running together considerations from mathematics, biology and ethics. While this multidisciplinary approach may contribute to the bold and rich character of their ideas, we can agree with Aristotle that such an approach lacks discipline and so does not represent a desirable ideal of mature science, whatever initial heuristic value it may have.[42] Aristotle pondered the lessons that these early and inchoate attempts at scientific explanation provided. His own, immensely influential, ideal of scientific specialism was provoked by reflection on these lessons.

Thus any proper understanding of Aristotle's philosophy must recognise the intimate connection between it and the intellectual background from which it sprang. Aristotle acknowledged this fundamental feature of his philosophical method; and even if his theorising about it did not mesh with his practice, it would still be of considerable interest as a piece of metaphilosophy. In fact, his diagnosis of his own practice is accurate; and I have illustrated, in the case of three pervasive topics, how the background of his predecessors' work determines Aristotle's thoughts about his own task.

So far I have said little about how he executes the task, except in relation to his theory of philosophy. But we already know more than we might have, and for two reasons. First, the practice of his philosophy will follow from the theory; secondly, the detail of his own discussion of some particular topic will owe much to the kind of background views considered in this chapter.

In Chapter 2 we shall examine three passages which reveal a great deal about Aristotle's substantive philosophical views. In the process we shall learn more about philosophy in the Aristotelian style.

Notes

1 *E.N.* K2, 1173al.
2 *Critique of Pure Reason* B395.
3 For example, A.J. Ayer, *The Problem of Knowledge* (London, 1956),

pp.7-8; B. Russell, *The Problems of Philosophy* (Oxford, 1967), p.91.

4 Both views are well expounded by P.H. Nowell-Smith, *Ethics* (London, 1954), pp.11-22.

5 'Philosophy' in the modern sense, that is. He does use a word which is transliterated 'philosophy'; but this tends to be reserved for the study which he pursues in the *Metaphysics* (see *Met.* K3, 1061b3-11) and is clearly narrower than our term.

6 *Met.* B1, 995b4-6a17; see W.D. Ross, *Aristotle's Metaphysics*, vol.1 (Oxford, 1924), pp.221-5.

7 *Met.* B1, 995a27-33; cf. *E.N.* H2, 1146a24-7.

8 *Meno* 85d5-e5; for Aristotle's interest in the lazy argument of the *Meno*, cf. *An. Post.* A1, 71a24-30.

9 See especially *An. Post.* A1-3, 10, B3-7, 19, and J. Barnes, 'Aristotle's Theory of Demonstration', *Phronesis* 14 (1969), 123-52.

10 The introductions to the discussions of place (*Phys.* Δ1, 208a27-9) and time (*Phys.* Δ10, 217b29-33) provide one out of many examples of discussions which echo the themes of *An. Post.*; see P. Moraux, 'La méthode d'Aristote dans l'étude du ciel', in S. Mansion (ed.), *Aristote et les Problèmes de Méthode* (Louvain, 1961), pp.173-94.

11 *Top.* A2; *An. Post.* A11, 77a26-35.

12 For a full discussion of dialectic, see my *Aristotle's Concept of Dialectic* (Cambridge, 1977).

13 W.V. Quine, 'Two Dogmas of Empiricism', in *From a Logical Point of View* (New York, 1953), pp.42-6.

14 This is convincingly argued by H. Cherniss, *The Riddle of the Early Academy* (New York, 1962).

15 *G.C.* A8, 325a18-23.

16 Plato *Republic* 476c2-7; cf. *Timaeus* 51d5-7.

17 Some specimen texts for this fundamental doctrine of Plato: *Phaedo* 65d-6a, 100a; *Symposium* 211a1-b5; *Republic* 596a4-6; *Parmenides* 130e5-1a2. See I.M. Crombie, *An Examination of Plato's Doctrines*, vol.2 (London, 1963), pp.247-52.

18 Plato *Parmenides* 132a, d-e; Aristotle *De Ideis* fr.4.

19 *Cat.* 7, 6b6-11.

20 *Met.* A9, 990b16; *De Ideis* fr.4.

21 At *Rep.* 523e, 524c he recognises the relativity of context in judgements about the size of physical objects, but reckons that precisely this tells against the adequacy of the concept of largeness employed in such judgements.

22 Plato's anticipation of Aristotle's theory of categories, with his distinction between absolute and relative at *Sophist* 255c12-13, has long been recognised; see G.E.L. Owen, 'A Proof in the *Peri Ideon*', repr. in R.E. Allen (ed.), *Studies in Plato's Metaphysics* (London, 1965), p.304.

23 *Met.* B2, 997b5-34 develops this difficulty in detail for various studies and their objects.

24 *Met.* A9, 990b1-8.

25 This defence is suggested by the argument of *Republic* 597c-d.

[26] *Met*. A3, 983b6-18.
[27] cf. *Phys*. A4, 188a17-18.
[28] *Met*. A7, 988a22-35.
[29] Aristotle attributes reasoning of this sort to earlier thinkers, probably including Anaximander (*Phys*. Γ5, 204b 22-9); cf. the distinction between E-substances and C-substances in the interpretation of Anaxagoras by C. Strang, 'The Physical Theory of Anaxagoras', *Archiv für Geschichte der Philosophie* 45 (1963), 101-3.
[30] *Met*. A9, 991a8-23; *G.C.* B9, 335b9-24.
[31] *P.A*. A1, 640a10-19.
[32] This is the fundamental criticism of the strategy of studying biology by a schematic division of natural kinds (*P.A*. A2-4, esp. 642b10-20). Plato is sometimes taken not to be a target of this criticism; but even though other members of the Academy doubtless developed the method of division in particular directions, the examples of it given in the *Sophist* and *Politicus* provide the original impetus for these developments.
[33] cf. *Met*. Z11, 1036b3-32.
[34] *Phys*. A4, 187a26-b1; cf. *G.C.* A1, 314a8-16, b1-15a2.
[35] *Phys*. A7, 190b3-13; A9, 192a8-16.
[36] *Gorgias* 449d-50b; *Philebus* 56c-7e; and there are extended examples of such classifications in the *Sophist* and *Politicus*.
[37] *Republic* 533-4; *Philebus* 57e-8a.
[38] *S.E.* 11, 172a13-15; *An. Post*. B7, 92b13-14; *Met*. B3, 998b22.
[39] *S.E.* 11, 172a8-9.
[40] *G.A*. B8, 747b27-8a12.
[41] *G.A*. B8, 748a15-9a7.
[42] Cf. his criticism of the Pythagoreans, *Met*. A8, 989b29-90a29.

CHAPTER 2

Aristotelian Method

Contemporary philosophers and scholars of philosophy sometimes complain that there is something fundamental missing from Aristotle's discussion of a particular topic. As serious practitioners of their trade they feel obliged to learn from what Aristotle says, and they are intrigued by the details of his insights. But the perspective of twentieth-century philosophy differs from Aristotle's in certain ways; and it is not surprising—indeed only natural—if some things that matter very much in current analysis of a problem should be altogether unrecognised by Aristotle.

Such complaint is plausible, but wrong. He has in fact considered the matters he is accused of neglecting, and has said important things about them. We read Aristotle to learn from him, and the lessons will impress us more if the divergences between his views and ours are settled mainly in our favour. Of course, some of the learning process will go the other way, or the enterprise would be without philosophical substance. So the honest philosopher will admit in principle—even if he will not readily concede it in practice—that Aristotle may be more right than current orthodoxy allows.

The ultimate standard in the debate will have to be current philosophy. Sometimes, where current orthodoxy declares Aristotle to be wrong—or worse, silent—I shall say that he is right. And if these claims are true, they will not be obviously so. To sustain them will be a matter partly for scholarship and partly for philosophy: it will consist in bringing neglected texts to the centre of attention, and in nudging philosophical thought into slightly new channels. The discussions we shall now consider are powerful enough to do this.

One of the most distinctive marks of philosophy since Descartes has been its concern with the foundations of knowledge. Reflection on this topic has led some to scepticism. It has led others to the view that philosophy can do no more than analyse the concepts employed in judgements; so philosophers lack the competence to advance or reject substantive judgements on the issues involved. Such dominant features of post-Cartesian philosophy seem to be missing from the Greeks. That this is a false appearance will become clear from the following examination of three Aristotelian discussions. My first and third examples come from his moral philosophy, while the second is from his philosophy of mind.

The Goal in Life

Aristotle's ethics is a prescription for a good human life. His purpose is that his audience should acquire the practical skill of living well and happily.[1] Much modern moral philosophy would be sceptical of this enterprise; it seems to ignore the subjectivity of morality. Morality must respect the autonomy of each agent's will or it mistakes its subject matter. But persons can differ in their fundamental moral concerns; and so any moral prescription must be relative to the individuals involved. Since relativism is apparently incompatible with general and universal formulae for the good life, Aristotle's programme seems threatened. Worse, he seems unaware of the difficulty.[2]

But he is aware of it. He devotes to this topic one of the most penetrating contributions to the metaphysic of morals. It comes in a discussion of wishing and its object.[3] The crucial passage is brief and deceptively easy:

> I have said that wishing is for the end; but it seems to some to be for what is good, and to others to be for what appears good. The result is that for those who say that the good is the object of wish, what is wished by one who does not choose correctly is not an object of wish (for if it is an object of wish, it will also be good; yet as things have turned out, it was bad),—and again for those who say that what appears good is the object of wish, there is not a natural object of wish, but for each person it is what it seems to be; yet different things appear so to different people, and it may turn out that these things are opposite. Now if these results are unsatisfactory, we should say that the good is simply and in truth the object of wish,

> but what appears good is the object of each person's wish—and what is in truth the object of wish is so for the virtuous person, while for the bad person it is up to chance. (*E.N.* Γ4, 1113a15-26)

When Aristotle discusses wishing and its object, he is examining a person's ultimate and fundamental criteria of value as expressed in his general aim in life. So in my further comments on his problem and the various answers to it, I shall vary the idiom slightly and talk in terms of a person's 'goal in life'.

What can be said about the ultimate goal in life? It may seem that at least we can say that the goal is the good life. Everyone would reply, if asked what sort of life he wanted, that the life should be good. But this may be no more significant than the agreement which we could also discover if we asked each person who he was. The unanimity in the answer 'me' is illusory, since it cannot be taken to prove that everyone is the same person; in the same way, the relativist claims, there is only superficial unanimity in the universally expressed preference for the good life. Probe further what each respondent means by this and you will find no significant convergence among the various aims that individual persons have. It may be then that a truer way to characterise the ultimate goal is: what appears to the individual to be the good life. This will preserve, as the first suggestion does not, the diversity of aims among autonomous moral agents.

Aristotle's discussion in *E.N.* Γ starts from the conflict between these two approaches to the problem. He notes that each can be supported in the way indicated, and yet that each also leads to unacceptable consequences. Moreover, the reason why each is unacceptable is fundamentally the same. Neither answer can sustain our conviction that the goals of some people are better than those of others.

If we maintain that people's goal is the good life, we are faced with the problem of explaining how someone could choose a life that is in fact bad, and set himself this as the goal. It is irrelevant whether he thinks of it as good or bad; if in fact the life prescribed is a bad one, then his aim is directed at something other than the good life. But in that case his goal would be what this account rules out as a possible goal, given its thesis that the goal is the good life. So nobody can have a bad goal; as a matter of logic, everyone must be as sound in his aim as is everybody else.

The proponent of the alternative answer may seize on this talk about aim to introduce what he takes to be important: the question of how things appear, how the good life exists subjectively.[4] We may agree that everyone aims at what appears to him to be the good life; to characterise the apparent good as the universal goal will not exclude the individual agents whose goal is bad. This answer, then, appears to avoid the pitfall of the first answer.

But the upshot is the same. If every agent is equally set in his aim on the goal in life, then we are deprived of the means to grade different individuals, and their aims, according to how well or badly they are directed towards their goal. Once again we reach the conclusion that anyone who has an ultimate goal is, as a matter of logic, certain to attain it. For every agent's aim is equally directed towards what the second account prescribes as the goal in life, since this is what each agent takes to be the good. This second account works in on the problem from the opposite end to that of the first account. It starts from subjective considerations, from a recognition of the need to attend to the aims of the individuals with goals. But it concludes that each of these aims is successful. Its conclusion is, therefore, indistinguishable from that of the account which starts from the opposite end of the phenomenon. The first account concentrated on the objective character of the goal of life, from the premise that this is the good life; it concludes that only those individuals who have this aim in their sights can strictly be aiming at the goal at all.

An absolutist conception of moral value—one that sets the same standard for all agents—will clearly undermine itself if it cannot provide a moral grading of the aims that different individuals have. Equally the relativist, seeking to allow for the crucial role played by the will of the individual agent in establishing moral value, destroys his own enterprise if he deprives himself of the possibility of assigning different values to different kinds of will. Only the sceptic can take comfort from the result of the discussion. But since the most plausible argument for moral scepticism is based on the relativity of persons, the attractiveness of scepticism is reduced to the extent that its basis in relativism is shown to be defective.

Aristotle thinks that all parties to this debate are hampered by an oversimple view of the relation between an agent and his goal. He engages in conceptual analysis and introduces a distinction which the other parties seem unaware of. On this basis, he is also able to advance a substantive thesis about the goals that people should have in life.

The analytical distinction points out a complexity in the concept of being a goal in life. We may speak of such goals in an absolute and unqualified way or we may qualify them by reference to the individual whose life it is. There is the goal in life and the goal in so-and-so's life. Armed with this distinction, we can see that the original two answers to the question about the nature of the goal are not, as might easily be supposed, incompatible. If we consider the matter generally and without reference to individuals, the first answer is correct. The unanimity of everyone's response to the question, their agreement in nominating the good life, justifies us in characterising the good life as the general and unqualified goal. But we notice divergences in detail when we inspect the goals of individual people, and so we find support for the second answer. It is what each person supposes to be the good life that determines his own goal. The characterisation of the goal as the apparent good is justified when we qualify the concept of the goal in life by mentioning some particular person whose life—and goal—is in question.

But this is only half of Aristotle's account. If he had left the matter here, he would have offered the competing parties a means of resolving the dispute. There is no guarantee that they would accept the offer. Either protagonist might decide to dig in and reject the other component in Aristotle's composite account. The relativist who originally championed the view that the goal in life is the apparent good, could resist the idea that the good is any part of the correct account—even in the sense of being a general and unqualified goal. He could say that every life is the life of an individual agent; and so in a proper analysis the only goal that matters is what each such agent sets himself. From this position, only one form of the concept of a goal in life should appear in a serious analysis: this is the concept of the qualified and person-relative goal. So Aristotle needs to say more to rescue his account from the charge of blandness. And he does.

The crucial further step is to say that the good is not merely the *unqualified* goal in life but also the *true* goal. It is the true goal because it is the goal that the good man pursues in life. It is, therefore, wrong to see the unqualified goal in life as something general and unspecified, since it is also something highly specific: it is what, in detail, the good man pursues. However, what he pursues is, in a way, what everyone pursues. On the other hand, the goal of someone other than the good man is not, in any sense, the goal in life; it is only the goal in *his* life.

This second half of his account shows Aristotle in agreement with those who maintain that there is more than a purely formal and superficial unity to the goal in life. There is substantive unity because it is a prescription for an actual life, that of the good person. But we found that those who wanted to support this position could not do so, because they would have to pay the inordinately high price of denying other kinds of person any goal at all. Aristotle's account avoids this sacrifice by employing a richer conception of a goal in life, according to which the other kinds of person do indeed have goals; only, they are not to be identified with the goal, nor to be allowed to stand as goals without further qualification. In this way Aristotle can incorporate the relativists' recognition of the importance of the individual agent in determining the nature of the goal, without going to the unacceptable extreme of making each and every such determination equal in its moral significance.

Aristotle's positive thesis is not surprising or paradoxical. To be sure, not everyone would agree with it; and there is a certain kind of opponent—one who would deny that there is any moral difference between the goals people have—whose position seems to be quite untouched by Aristotle's analysis and argument. He is interested in reaching a more significant audience; these are thinkers, like the authors of the first two accounts of the goal in life, who want to give an account of the moral significance of different lives but, it turns out, cannot do so for lack of adequate conceptual analysis. Frustrated in this way they are liable to be diverted to a position at variance with Aristotle's substantive claim that the goal in life is what the good man pursues. Aristotle rescues this platitude from the paradoxical conclusions to which the proponents of the first two answers are propelled; at the same time he provides a corrective to arguments aiming directly for such conclusions. In this somewhat indirect manner his argument answers the moral sceptic who thinks it wrong or impossible to establish the existence of differences in moral evaluation.

Here we have a contribution to the metaphysic of morals, a discussion whose significance can easily be missed because Aristotle casts it in the form of a response to a specific dilemma. Yet when we reflect on the import of the discussion, we can see that it is an effective setting for approaching the problem. Aristotle uses an arresting clash of views to ease us into a deeply difficult issue in moral theory. Unlike many later philosophers he does not plunge us straight into a statement of a contentious metaphysical position. The whole discussion is an excellent illustration of his philosophical method, as well as being a notable tour de force of analysis.

Psychophysical Properties

The second example of Aristotle's philosophical method comes from his work in the philosophy of mind. It used to be thought that Aristotle ignored the mind–body problem.[5] This charge has become no longer tenable as philosophers have noted the connections between his work and recent versions of physicalism. But he is still faulted for tending to treat psychology simply as a branch of biology and for ignoring what must be a central topic for a properly philosophical approach—the nature of consciousness.[6] Those who find this charge persuasive should ponder a passage near the beginning of the *De Anima*, where Aristotle is assembling methodological considerations which bear on the investigation of the human soul, i.e. the person. Alerting us to the need to consider bodily features in this context, he says:

> The affections of a soul seem all to occur with a body—spiritedness, gentleness, terror, pity, daring, also joy and loving and hating: the body is affected at the same time as these. Evidence of this is that sometimes people are not at all stirred or terrified when violent and vivid affections occur, and on occasion they are moved by slight and feeble affections, when the body rages and is in the state that it is in when it is enraged. A case that is clearer still: when nothing terrifying is occurring people become affected in the manner of one who is terrified. (*De An*. A1. 403a16-24)

At first glance the passage seems to convey sound psychosomatic doctrine. The first sentence makes the general point about the connection between a given psychological affection—terror or whatever—and a physical one. The psychological state of terror correlates, we may suppose, with some such physical state as cold sweat breaking out on the skin. The second and third sentences then provide examples of such correlations.

Here is the difficulty. What we get—or rather what is hinted at—are not so much examples as counter-examples. The phenomena to which Aristotle alludes in support of his general psychosomatic principle seem to represent cases in which the psychological and bodily affections come apart. They provide the worst possible support for the thesis that psychological affections correlate with the physical. Once we see this difficulty, we can also find additional problems in the examples provided in these sentences. In particular it is unclear what kinds of thing—psychological or physical—are the subjects of the verbs used here. Take the second sentence: what, in terms of the psychological/physical divide, is it that is not terrified, and what undergoes the vivid affections? Does Aristotle mean that 'rages' and 'is enraged' are properties of physical entities? It seems so; yet surely in a discussion that purports to be about psychological matters 'is enraged' must be construed as a psychological predicate.

Before we try to resolve these problems, one feature of contemporary discussions of mind–body relations needs to be set aside. A type/token distinction can be used to support the claim that while there is no general correlation between states of mind and states of body, still each particular physical state is identical to a particular psychological state.[7] This idea is unhelpful, at least for the initial approach to Aristotle's discussion. He works with no such distinction, and everything he says should be construed as applying indifferently both to general affections of soul or body and to the particular instantiations of such affections. The problem we have just raised should be seen as applying at both these levels. Despite this, it will emerge that his remarks here bear significantly on the strategies of those who have made much of the type/token distinction in the philosophy of mind.

Our starting point must rather be this. We acknowledge that

the proper understanding and characterisation of personal states, such as spiritedness, will involve both psychological and somatic factors. What remains to be resolved is whether either item in this setting of the problem has priority. Even to set the problem this way suggests that the answer will be 'yes'. The very approach seems dualistic; and if this is only an implication, to be dispelled by analysis, hard work will be necessary if the outcome is to be monism.

Let us look more closely at Aristotle's examples. In at least some of them, clearly, we are dealing with bodily changes that are not accompanied by the normal psychological changes. Thus the body may be in a state that would be normally counted as a case of anger, but the psychological components of anger are missing. The reverse may also happen. There may be no bodily reaction even though the psychological features are present. We learn more about the psychological dimension from the final example. When Aristotle says that nothing terrifying is occurring, he is not trying to characterise the external world. For someone might have a mistaken view of this; he would feel terrified and quite unsurprisingly 'become affected in the manner of one who is terrified'. The 'occurrence of something terrifying' must refer to the feeling and awareness of terror. In the case that impresses Aristotle here, something characteristic of terror affects the person, but there is no feeling or awareness of terror.

Suppose that the psychosomatic approach is broadly correct. Then when we speak of what a person does or undergoes, it will not normally affect the truth of such a claim whether we interpret it as being about a body or about a mind. There will be a large measure of extensional equivalence between sentences that explicitly cast their claims in either of these two idioms. When such translations are spelled out, there may be some loss of naturalness, some lessening of intuitive appeal. Sentences of the form 'a person fears X'—for example, 'a person fears the Loch Ness monster' or 'a person fears that the Loch Ness monster will devour him'—may sound odd if we substitute 'a body' or 'a mind' for 'a person'. But this sense of oddness may be merely prejudice. Perhaps the prejudice will evaporate if we notice that on all occasions these substitutions preserve truth.

Aristotle encourages this interpretation by speaking of the body that 'rages' and is like one that 'is enraged'. Such language is music to the ears of the psychosomatic theorist. It is indicative of a state of affairs which he declares to be universal; in the world as he conceives it, the properties of persons are borne by subjects which can be identified indifferently as either minds or bodies. In particular, the only possible subject which can bear predicates ascribing such properties as awareness or feeling, is physical in character. We must, then, simply adjust to the idea that bodies can feel fear or anger. Initial intuitions to the contrary should not obstruct the development of this truer insight.

Why should Aristotle discourage this approach too? Essentially because it oversimplifies. In his day, as now, there were thinkers who could not accept that the facts of consciousness could be reduced to purely physical terms. Most notably, Plato and the Pythagoreans argued in favour of the soul as a seat of consciousness which was quite independent of the body.[8] So thoroughly was Plato committed to this view that he readily degraded sense-perception to a level below that of full consciousness; sense-perception involves the body and is therefore disqualified. Plato argued in this way;[9] Descartes followed him, and Kripke maintains the tradition today.[10] Plainly this tradition has robust powers of resistance against argument—let alone the mere assertion—that states of consciousness are really only states of the brain and other parts of the bodily system.

So Aristotle proceeds more cautiously; and his strategy is twofold. First, he investigates certain cases which seem to favour the dualist; he urges us to see these cases as non-standard and exceptional. Secondly, he shows how our natural habits of thought and talk, even as they are applied to such cases, support a monist interpretation of the connection between mind and body.

The first phase of the strategy invites us to reflect on how the exception proves the rule. If dualism were correct, why should we be surprised that in some cases mental phenomena are not accompanied by bodily affections, or vice versa? Even if such accompaniments are frequent, this is not of much significance in itself; and the dualist bases his argument on the lack of necessity for the coexistence of the two kinds of event. But we ought to be at least as impressed by the frequent, normal cases as by the rare, exceptional cases. It is surely reasonable strategy to understand the unitary subject, indicated by the normal cases, as the true subject of personal properties; and we shall adjust our understanding and description of the exceptional cases accordingly.

This adjustment is considered in the second phase. The character of the exceptional cases is captured precisely by attributing to the body the psychological properties which are said not to occur. When we say that the body is in a state of fear even though there is no feeling of fear, this is to deny that there is fear. Yet the most accurate and informative way to speak of the bodily state is to use the notion of fear. Even in cases which seem to put the monist thesis under strain, the language of monism is the most appropriate way to characterise them. Aristotle infers that monism is the conceptually basic scheme. While the exceptional cases show that this conceptual scheme needs sensitive interpretation and application, they do nothing to justify its abandonment. The reverse is the proper lesson.

Modern psychophysicalists have argued that a theory which maintains that each token psychological state is identical with a physical state, might not be able to provide defensible correlations between types of psychological and physical states. So monism can be sustained even if we lack such general correlations. Aristotle's discussion suggests he would regard this strategy as unnecessarily defeatist. A general, type-level psychophysical correlation is not refuted simply by the discovery of some counter-instances. We can maintain detailed psychophysical laws consistently with countenancing such exceptions. Whether in fact there are such laws is of course a matter for empirical investigation. Aristotle thinks he has discovered some; and modern science makes similar claims. Modern psychophysical philosophers do not dispute the scientific claim, only its philosophical interpretation.[11] Aristotle provides an argument which makes contact with their scepticism.

This brief passage in the *De Anima* looked unpromising at first, but it has yielded much. On closer inspection it combines insights into the physiology of human life with an unmistakably philosophical concern to explore the facts of consciousness. The charge that Aristotle neglects consciousness thus fails. The passage also provides important insights into method in the philosophy of mind. Aristotle draws on ordinary habits of thought to support a position which confronts a philosophical paradox—the paradox of dualistic theory. He scrutinises our normal ways of thinking and talking, and the examination enables him to explain why some have found this paradox plausible. He insists that we shall be guided towards the truth only by holding on to what ordinary language already indicates: the phenomena which impress the dualist are exceptions to the normal. The structure of Aristotle's argument depends thoroughly on its manner of leading us to a conclusion through attention to the available views.

Ambition

The third example of Aristotle's philosophical method comes once again from ethics. A commonplace of modern moral philosophy is the need to observe the distinction between metaethics and moralising. The latter activity issues in directives and prescriptions to act and not to act in certain ways. The layman will naturally suppose that discovering such directives must be what moral philosophy is about. But many philosophers would disagree. They profess to pursue metaethics; this is an investigation into the nature and evidential status of moral judgements, and is conceived as mostly neutral regarding the truth or falsity of the moralist's prescriptions. Sometimes these approaches are contrasted as being first-order and second-order. Even when not completely eschewing first-order moral thought and debate, modern moral philosophers typically regard such practical ethics as quite distinct from the metaethical dimension of moral philosophy.

Aristotle's work contains no trace of any such distinction. Some have regarded his moral philosophy as seriously deficient on this score;[12] but perhaps we should draw the opposite lesson—that the distinction is ill-conceived. This would be Aristotle's comment on it, I believe; and a passage to be considered shortly will provide a detailed illustration of the kind of moral philosophy which results if we ignore the distinction.

He does not comment directly on the contrast between metaethics and moralising, but he does reject a closely related attempt to mount a conception of moral philosophy which anticipates this division. This is Plato's theory of moral value. Plato held that the source of the highest value is an unchanging and purely intelligible entity—the Form of Good. To conceive value in this way will result in prescribing as a goal a life of contemplation rather than a life of action; moreover, the exercise of thought in such a life will in no way be directed towards action. Plato's moral philosophy is, of course, full of directives to act in various ways. But the unmistakable tendency of his thought is to direct us towards an ideal state of affairs in which the need for, or even the possibility of, action has been eliminated.[13]

The motivation for Plato's theory is a wish to avoid the sceptical relativism that results from a view of moral value as liable to variation in different circumstances. This has already been mentioned earlier in the examination of Aristotle's discussion of the goal in life. Although Aristotle sympathises with Plato's motivation, he does not accept the theory which Plato derives from it. He agrees that the best life for a person must consist of thought, but insists against Plato that since a person is more than just a mind, the thought must be directed towards action.[14] Practical thought differs fundamentally from theoretical thought which has as its only aim the contemplation of truth; the one cannot be reduced to the other. Despite his emphasis on the practical character of such thought, Aristotle opposes any suggestion that human action should be based on something other than thought. Anti-intellectualism in the philosophy of action misrepresents its subject just as much as does the Platonic attempt wholly to divorce reason from action. Reason is the foundation of action and it is a form of reason that is practical through and through.[15]

When Aristotle opposes the immobilism of Plato's theory, he is offering grounds which also tell against a metaethical, action-neutral conception of moral philosophy. Such theorising does not have built into its form that it should issue in particular actions; so he cannot accept it as an exercise of practical reason. At the same time he rejects a conception of purely first-order, practical moralising. That would lack the basis in reason that is required by his idea of moral action. He refuses to endorse either Plato's intellectualism or the emotivism which is diametrically opposed to it; and to take this view is to refuse to divide moral philosophy into metaethics and moralising.

An excellent illustration of how theory and practice are connected is provided by his doctrine of the mean.[16] It is an account of the virtues and vices of character, of how we should regulate our actions and feelings so as to avoid both overdoing and underdoing things. It is thus both thoroughly practical in intention—designed to bring about right dispositions in people who understand it—and also theoretical; and it is theoretical in the double sense of being a theory about dispositions and of being an account of the reasoning involved in action. Yet much of the detailed discussion, where Aristotle tries to chart the positions of virtuous and vicious dispositions in terms of the three notions of excess, mean amount, and deficiency, may seem too bland and uncontentious to be regarded as a guide to action. Thus cowardice and recklessness are to be avoided as, respectively, an excess and a deficiency in the regulation of the emotion of fear; in between lies the commendable disposition of courage. Again, in conversational exchange, we are told that buffoonery and boorishness are the excess and the deficiency, while wittiness is the mean. So obvious are the moral insights expressed in these judgements that the very terms used to express them carry an incontestable connotation of praise or blame.

Reflection on these parts of the theory of the mean can easily persuade us that it is a piece of conceptual analysis—of metaethics—rather than a positive prescription for the good life. The following passage on ambition should give us pause:

> It is possible to desire office both more and less than one ought to. The person who is excessive in his desires is called ambitious, he who is defective is called unambitious, and the middle type lacks a name. The dispositions are also nameless except that of the ambitious person, which is ambition. Because of this the extremes lay claim to the middle territory. We sometimes call the middle type ambitious, sometimes unambitious; and sometimes we praise the ambitious person, sometimes the unambitious person. (*E.N.* B7, 1107b27-1108a1)

Aristotle's linguistic observations, although made in and about Greek, also apply with remarkable accuracy to English. We too feel that there is a tension in our use of the terms 'ambitious' and 'unambitious' to characterise dispositions. Each contains an uneasy combination of the commendatory and the pejorative; and the reason is clear. As Aristotle says, we are inclined to regard these dispositions as both good and bad.

We have a conceptual problem; we must untangle these evaluations to reach a clear and determinate answer to the question of whether and why it is good to be ambitious or unambitious. At the same time there is plainly a practical problem of some urgency. Each of us is liable to be faced with particular decisions about whether or not to seek office—and to what lengths we should go. For Aristotle has in mind not so much major offices of state as offices in small organisations, such as clubs and societies. Are we to be ambitious or unambitious? Which disposition is to be pursued and which avoided? Neither answer seems to be clearly right or wrong, and neither to be more right than wrong. Moreover the conceptual and the practical problems are not just connected; they are obviously the same problem, and any solution to the problem in one of its aspects will serve for the other aspect too.

Aristotle's leading idea for a solution is derived directly from his theory of the mean. With any kind of action there are three possible dispositions. But in the present case our normal linguistic resources provide labels for no more than two. This is both a symptom and a cause of a parallel conceptual limitation. It naturally occurs to us to suppose that there are just two ways in matters of office that a person can be disposed—ambitious and unambitious. Reflection on the theory of the mean shows that this is a mistake. There are three possible dispositions; two are wrong through excess and deficiency, and one is right.

If these are the facts of the matter, there will be two ways in which they can be misunderstood. It may be supposed that one of the two characters—the ambitious or the unambitious—must be praiseworthy; and the problem will be to settle which it is. On the other hand, we may recoil from the obviously blameworthy quality of both dispositions; and then we shall be at a loss to know what further stance we could take. Either way we shall tend to gravitate towards the extremes, setting in train the process of habituation by which the extremes come to seem to embody morally valuable dispositions.

Aristotle considers it natural for people to incline towards the extremes, and one of the chief purposes of the theory of the mean is to correct the tendency.[17] It will be particularly helpful with actions where there exists no distinct name for the mean disposition, as in the pursuit of office. He shows that there is a way to avoid being unambitious without espousing the unacceptable alternative of being ambitious; similarly those who wish to avoid being ambitious are not forced to become unambitious. Not only that: Aristotle also indicates how both unacceptable extremes can be avoided and a correct disposition can be cultivated as we carry on the practice of our lives.

More specific guidance is not possible, given the general and abstract level at which Aristotle must operate as he addresses all reasonable men.[18] But the discussion of ambition is not pitched at a level which is too abstract to be practically useful. Such a claim might have seemed doubtful if we had only such examples as courage, cowardice and recklessness. But as we learn from the case of ambition, there is useful work for the theory of the mean to do, even though it must abstract from the particularities of individual agents.

This lesson carries important implications for the case of courage too. It would be a mistake to suppose that this virtue is more easily attainable just because we have a name for it. The world may be full of people who are cautious and people who are daring. Suppose they all agree in praising courage and disagree only in what they count as courage. The cautious people blame what the daring people praise, calling it recklessness; and the daring blame what the cautious praise, calling that cowardice. Their agreement in praising courage is revealed as empty; and the situation is only formally different from that of the people who divide into the ambitious and the unambitious.

There is indeed a difference. This is the availability of the word 'courage', which is used by both parties as a term of commendation. But in the above scenario this measure of agreement is of almost no moral significance. That is why Aristotle is right not to propose, in response to the difficulties about the pursuit of office, that some term should be coined for the mean virtuous disposition, in order to confine 'ambition' and 'unambition' to the pejorative role of designating the vicious extremes.[19] If we had such a term, it would make it only marginally easier to understand that this disposition is the one to be pursued. Indeed it might impede moral progress. If people possessed an unproblematic vocabulary for praiseworthy and blameworthy dispositions, they might be led to believe that virtue is more easily attainable than it is. Just so do the cowards and the reckless take themselves to be courageous—an easy option in view of the availability of this term for commendation.

The example of ambition is so useful precisely because it precludes this easy option. It is not obvious what is wrong with the extremes, or even that anything is wrong with them. If Aristotle is correct about ambition, his audience will only achieve a grasp of the mean by a long, careful process of habituation and development of insight. Once we see this here, the message carries over to the other dispositions too. We see the purpose and practical importance of the theory of the mean as a whole. The discussion of ambition clarifies the nature of the theory and offers help in the business of living. It thus confirms my claim that in Aristotle's moral philosophy the task of conceptual analysis and the practical direction of agents in their choices in life form a seamless web.

The theory of the mean has a further and wider significance in Aristotle's thought. Although restricted in scope to the analysis of dispositions of character in respect of actions and emotions, it provides a model that can be extended for handling a great many other problems. There is a pattern common to all the discussions of the present chapter and of Chapter 1. In every case we have started from a position in which two opposed accounts of some question seem to have exhausted the possible positions and yet have thrown up difficulties which are both irresoluble and at root the same. This has been so in the case of the goal in life and the relation between mind and body, where the problems were set by the opposition between two readily available views. The same dialectical impasse guided our discussion of the general aim of philosophy. Is philosophy continuous with science, or does it have its own distinctive subject matter? Again, there is a conflict between the tendency to divide intellectual enquiry into specialised and autonomous departments, and the generalist recognition of common elements that run through the proper treatment of any philosophical problem.

Aristotle's method is to discover a middle way between the extreme positions that have served to set up the problem. The beginning of intellectual rectitude is to see the need to avoid each of the extremes; and philosophical dexterity assists the learner to work out in detail how to attain a middle course, which alone is free from paradox. Aristotle goes to work on an audience of philosophers who are committed to one or other of the extreme positions: the philosophers are analogous to moral agents who see no difficulty in their desire to be either ambitious or unambitious. A first step in addressing the latter is to confront each party with the opposite kind of character, in the hope that he will recognise the symmetry of the other's position with his own. For exactly the same reason it is sound philosophical method to highlight the starkness of the opposition between two familiar views. The temptation to espouse either is likely to be lessened when it becomes apparent that the alternative is championed with the same fervour and, indeed, that it is beset by some of the same difficulties. If the participants and the audience to a dispute are induced to see the matter in this way, they will be readier to recognise the need for some third position which avoids the extremes, and to go in search of it. The value and purpose of the third position is defined by the fact that it is distinct from the other two.

We have explored some leading features of the characteristically Aristotelian way of tackling a philosophical problem. At the same time we have begun to discover some substantive theses of his philosophy. These will be developed in the following chapters; and we shall frequently be reminded of the lessons we have learned about the purpose and methods of philosophical enquiry.

Notes

1. *E.N.* A2, 1094a18-24; A3, 1095a2-11; B2, 1103b26-31.
2. These criticisms are usefully voiced by T.H. Irwin, 'The Metaphysical and Psychological Basis of Aristotle's Ethics' in A.O. Rorty (ed.), *Essays on Aristotle's Ethics* (California, 1980), pp.35-53, and by J. Barnes in the Introduction to *Aristotle's Ethics* (Penguin, 1976), pp.26-7; but it will be clear that I do not agree with their answers.
3. This passage is discussed in my *Aristotle's Concept of Dialectic* (Cambridge, 1977), pp.53-68; and it has also been examined by N.P. White, 'Goodness and Human Aims in Aristotle's Ethics' in D.J. O'Meara (ed.), *Studies in Aristotle* (Washington, 1981), pp.225-46. The present discussion differs in emphasis somewhat from my earlier one; here more weight is placed on those features of Aristotle's account which allow for the subjective elements in wishing.

4 We find this move at *Top.* Z8, 146b36-7a5.

5 D.W. Hamlyn, *Aristotle's De Anima, Books II and III* (Oxford, 1968), p.xiii.

6 See K.V. Wilkes, *Physicalism* (London, 1978), pp.114-35, although it must be said that she would not be happy about this way of formulating the point.

7 D. Davidson, 'Mental Events', in *Essays on Actions and Events* (Oxford, 1980), pp.207-25.

8 Plato *Phaedo* 83a-b. For the Pythagoreans, see W.K.C. Guthrie, *A History of Greek Philosophy*, vol.1 (Cambridge, 1962), pp.306-19.

9 *Phaedo* 79c-d.

10 S. Kripke, 'Naming and Necessity', in D. Davidson and G. Harman (eds.), *Semantics of Natural Language* (Dordrecht, 1972), pp.334-42.

11 See C. McGinn, 'Mental States, Natural Kinds and Psychophysical Laws', *Aristotelian Society Supplementary Volume* 52 (1978), pp.195-220.

12 J. Barnes, in the Introduction to *Aristotle's Ethics* (Penguin, 1976), pp.19-26.

13 Plato *Republic* 517c7-e2, 519d.

14 *E.N.* A6, 1096b31-7a13; *E.E.* A8, 1218b8-24.

15 *E.N.* A13, 1102b23-3a10; Z2.

16 For a general account of the doctrine, see *E.N.* B6-8. Useful commentary is provided by J.O. Urmson, 'Aristotle's Doctrine of the Mean', *American Philosophical Quarterly* 10 (1973), 223-30, and the reply by R. Hursthouse, 'A False Doctrine of the Mean', *Proceedings of the Aristotelian Society* 81 (1980-81), 57-72.

17 Cf. *E.N.* B6, 1106b28-35; B9, 1109a24-30.

18 *E.N.* B9, 1109b12-23; cf. the general remarks about the inevitable roughness of moral generalisation at B2, 1104a1-11. There is some valuable comment on this issue in R. Shiner, 'Ethical Perception in Aristotle', *Apeiron* 13 (1979), 79-85.

19 Aristotle recognises that many of the dispositions which the theory of the mean provides room for are anonymous, but no less real for that; *E.N.* Γ7, 1115b24-6. The more general philosophical lessons of this attitude to language are explored by R. Bambrough, 'Aristotle on Justice: A Paradigm of Philosophy', in R. Bambrough (ed.), *New Essays on Plato and Aristotle* (London, 1965), pp.159-74.

CHAPTER 3

Philosophy of Language

We all think ourselves familiar, both in philosophy and in ordinary thought, with the notion of a category. The idea has already been used in the discussion of Plato in Chapter 1, and his theories of reality and change were faulted by appeal to the notion of a category mistake. This form of confusion assimilates things which ought to be kept apart by anyone who shares our basic conceptual scheme. Different people know different things, and so some will make mistakes that others can easily avoid. But there is a certain kind of mistake that could not be made by anyone at all. For example, nobody could suppose that Thursday is blue or that generosity is oblong.[1] One could, of course, utter in the assertive mood a sentence containing these words; but we would immediately interpret this as a form of linguistic ignorance. What the utterer could not do would be to believe the statement which (as a matter of mistakable fact) the English sentence means.

Although category mistakes of the kind just given are impossible, some philosophers have detected category confusion in others who, they allege, have assimilated items which are not so obviously distinct. In this way someone may be accused of crossing the boundaries between categories if, for example, he treats numbers as objects, or objects as processes, or values as natural properties. Here the notion of a category mistake becomes more obscure; the charge imputes a latent, not a surface confusion, and it would usually be rejected by the person at whom it is levelled. We have moved beyond our initial idea of categories as tools for exposing nonsense.

Only two philosophers, Aristotle and Kant, have done original work in the theory of categories. Kant borrows much of Aristotle's terminology, but his theory is seemingly directed towards a very different task. Kant uses categories to analyse judgements and thereby to discover the *a priori* elements in all thought.[2] It is no easy matter to determine what Aristotle's theory is about; but it is certainly not what Kant's theory is about. Of the two, Aristotle's account has been by far the more influential. For the ancestry of the notion of a category confusion we look not to Kant but to Aristotle. So an examination of his discussion of categories may be expected to shed light on a topic which is far from clear.

I shall claim more. Philosophy of language looms large in contemporary philosophy; and a feature of Aristotle's work that makes it so rewarding an object to study is his evident interest in language. Dummett has recently argued that philosophical interest in language is not a simple phenomenon. He contrasts two styles of philosophy. The first is sensitive to linguistic accuracy with a view to avoiding ambiguity and generally achieving clarity of thought; the second aims unequivocally to derive ontological theory from an analysis of the basic elements of language. The first approach he associates with Austin and Wittgenstein and the second with Frege, and he is concerned particularly to emphasise the special character of Frege's programme for basing an account of reality on a correct grasp of the different functions which various linguistic items perform in expressing truth.[3]

There is no doubt that Aristotle has an Austinian interest in the fine distinctions revealed in ordinary talk. What has been less well recognised is that he also has a Fregean interest in using the basic distinctions between types of linguistic expression to serve as the ground for distinctions between the kinds of thing that exist. Nowhere is this ontological strategy more prominent than in the theory of categories.

The Theory of Categories

But this is to anticipate. First we shall see how Aristotle presents the theory and consider the problems which arise from this presentation. Only two passages even attempt a full account;

and they are rather different from each other. In the better known passage, *Categories* 4, he classifies and distinguishes what is signified by single units of language—that is, mainly, single words. Each such unit signifies either a substance or a quantity or a quality or a relative or somewhere or when or being in a position or having or doing or being affected. There follows a brief indication, through examples, of what the terms in this list mean. We shall be even briefer: a substance—a man; a quantity—two feet; a quality—white. The other passage is *Topics* A9. It presents virtually the same list and the same examples, but with one important difference. The first item in the list is not 'a substance' but 'what it is'; and even though the idea of substance makes its appearance later in the discussion, Aristotle does not amend the claim that the first item in the list of categories is *what it is*.

There is a further important divergence between the discussions of *Cat*. 4 and *Top*. A9. Whereas the former lists the items signified by uncombined words, the aim of the latter passage is to distinguish 'the kinds of predicate'. In fact it is only in the *Topics* that we get the Greek word of which 'category' is a transliteration: 'category' means a predicate.[4] This suggests that the *Topics* passage is likely to give us a deeper insight into the theory that we can derive from the *Categories*; and this will be important as our analysis develops.

First though, let us note a rather obvious roughness in Aristotle's list of categories. Consider, for example, 'a quantity', 'somewhere', 'being in a position'; the first of these suggests a certain kind of thing, the third a feature of a thing, and the second sits awkwardly between these interpretations. (Does it refer to a place, or to being in a place?) There is also a problem about the examples. Greek lacks the typographical device of quotation marks.[5] In many contexts it is unclear whether words are being used or mentioned. So when we find *a man* as an example of a substance, we cannot assume that this refers to a thing rather than to a piece of language.

The *Categories* provides our main detailed information about the theory; and yet its treatment suffers throughout from these obscurities. But let us postpone consideration of them until we have some material to work on.

The first category is substance, and Aristotle assigns it a

special position in relation to the others. They depend on substance for their existence.[6] In the *Categories*, but nowhere else, he draws a distinction between primary and secondary substances, which amounts to a contrast between individuals and the more or less general kinds under which they fall. The distinction is important for the evidence it provides for viewing substance as the primary bearer of predicates.[7]

Everything else is ultimately dependent on substance through one of two relations—being *said of* and being *present in*: substances are what the others are either said of or present in. The *said of* relation obtains between items of the same category, while the *present in* relation connects items in different categories. Aristotle maintains that these two relations underlie our indiscriminate use of the copula in predication; and he devises a test to determine which relation obtains in any given case. The test is linguistic. If we can replace the name of the item in question by its definition, then it is said of the subject; if not, it is present in it.[8]

The test is to be carried out on expressions that occur in the predicate position in a sentence. Thus 'a knight is a man' and 'a knight is brave' differ because in the first case the definition of the predicate term can be substituted for the term itself, but not in the second: the knight is an animal but not a virtue. So by the proposed criterion the item associated with the predicate term 'a man' is said of the subject, while the item associated with 'brave' is present in the subject.

The way Aristotle expresses his distinction—'said of' and 'present in'—seems to represent an uneasy combination of linguistic and ontological analysis. But it may be significant that the criterion used to differentiate actual examples of the relations is a linguistic one. We shall find that the same issues of interpretation arise with other parts of the theory.

Aristotle examines various criteria for distinguishing items in different categories; and some of these criteria get rejected in the course of the examination. Here are some examples of how this works. He makes much use of notions like variation in degree and possessing a contrary.[9] We say not merely that something is large but that it is more or less large than something else. This may come to saying that largeness itself can vary in degree, but this is not quite Aristotle's approach; he makes his point about variation in degree in terms of the predicate element in a sentence. Substances, on the other hand, cannot vary in degree. That is, if a man is a substance, then one thing cannot be more of a man than another is.

By applying a number of criteria of this kind and noting how they overlap and intersect to produce different kinds of predicate, Aristotle tries to produce a well-demarcated system for locating each predicate. His analysis contains some false starts and self-corrections which repay scrutiny. The discussion of the category of relatives is the most striking case. He starts with a criterion which appears to mark off a class of items successfully. Some things can only be spoken of in combination with some other thing; the linguistic expressions through which the items are presented are essentially incomplete. As Aristotle puts it, these things are always said *of* (or otherwise related to) something else: thus knowledge is knowledge of something and similarity is similarity to something. That is Aristotle's first definition of the items in this category.[10]

The difficulty is that while this criterion works well for many items that are relative, it lets in some further ones that clearly are not. Thus, when one thing is a part of another, it may be correct to speak of the first as being *of* the second; but there is better reason to assign the item to another category, not to that of relatives. A hand is someone's hand; money belongs to someone. But this should not oblige us to give up the view that such things are substances. A criterion which has the effect of assigning them to a different category is no good.

So Aristotle amends the criterion to the following: if something is relative, then for it to be what it is, is for it to be relative to something else.[11] He justifies this account by claiming that to understand the nature of something relative is to know what it is relative to. We must now consider how this revised definition affects our understanding of the general character of the theory of categories. The amendment in the definition of relatives is both instructive and baffling. The first criterion bears on the incompleteness of certain predicates; it is linguistic. Moreover it is natural to construe it as intended to classify items that are themselves linguistic. On this interpretation, predicates such as 'similar', 'a slave', will be distinguished by the fact that a supplement is required, either explicitly or implicitly from the surrounding context, if we are to have an adequate semantic unit. The second criterion has nothing linguistic about it. It is not a property of words that they should be relative to something else—except in the trivial sense that they occur next to each other, but this applies as much to substance-terms as to those in every other category. It seems clear that this criterion draws our attention to the things which are denoted by the relative terms, not to the terms themselves; those items which get classified as relative as a result of applying this criterion, will be ontological rather than linguistic.

Is the theory of categories an exercise in ontology or in linguistics? Does Aristotle classify things or words? Considerable support can be assembled for either answer. In defence of the ontological thesis, we have already noted how Aristotle uses the categories to support the claim that science must be articulated as reality is.[12] There is no single kind to which all things belong; and the simplest demonstration of this is by appeal to the irreducible differences between categories. Categories seem to be very general kinds into which things fall—that is, ontological kinds. In discussing the location of kinds within a system of classification by species and genus, Aristotle makes much use of categories.[13] One way of defeating a claim that two kinds are related as species and genus is to show that they are in different categories. Since he often connects this objection with the thesis that a species cannot belong to two distinct genera, it is natural to infer that the categories are very general kinds of thing under which other kinds—and ultimately all individuals—fall.

Other passages and contexts of discussion tell in favour of a linguistic interpretation. Aristotle frequently uses the categories to point up ambiguities that are liable to mislead us in philosophy. In one passage he comes very close to the contemporary appeal to the idea of a category mistake, when he discusses a particular kind of fallacious argument. *S.E.* 22 considers cases where similarity of verbal form may encourage the assumption that the words denote things of the same kind. To suppose that all nouns name a thing's nature, or that all active verbs denote an activity, is to invite confusion. The theory of categories articulates our sense that seeing is not an activity despite its being designated by a verb in the active voice; similarly, white is not the nature of anything even though the colour is named by a noun.[14]

This may seem a further use of the theory to promote ontological insight, but matters are not so simple. The names of the categories are terms of grammar, whatever else they may also be. The notions of activity, quality or time serve to distinguish and classify items and parts of language; they explain a semantic dimension in sentences. In exposing these mistakes Aristotle may wish to direct our attention from surface grammar towards an appreciation of the deeper grammatical realities. In that case, the lessons are that, despite appearances, 'to see' is not an active verb and 'white' is not the name of a colour. Those who make the mistakes about seeing and white are misled by the form of the expression; they are confused about the meanings of terms because they construe their grammar in the wrong way.[15]

From such considerations one might infer that the theory of categories is an essay in the analysis and classification of the elements of language. But this interpretation encounters difficulties too. The theory of categories is rather obviously incomplete as an account of the varieties of linguistic item. Only the major parts of speech—nouns, verbs, adjectives, some adverbs—are considered. Prepositions and conjunctions are ignored; and yet Aristotle knew that these could be important in the theory of meaning.[16] A further point is that the classification effected by the theory of categories cuts across grammatical distinctions. 'Justice' names an item in the category of quality, but the adjective 'just' also signifies the quality of a thing.[17] Clearly these two words belong together in what we may neutrally call the linguistic dimension of the theory of categories. But since a purely linguistic classification would surely separate these two words, this cannot be the aim of the theory.

Language and Reality

Both the ontological and the linguistic interpretations present difficulties; and it may seem that the problems in the latter exceed even those in the former. But this conclusion must be too quick; for, as we have noted, the theory of categories is a theory of predicates. We can get a clearer grasp of this, and of the import of the whole theory, from the relatively neglected discussion in *Topics* A9.[18] A major puzzle about this passage is that it seems to provide two incompatible accounts of the categories; and the divergence concerns the first category, the most important one.

When he introduces the list of categories in this passage, Aristotle uses the label 'what it is', or, as I shall render it, 'nature', for the first category. The rest of the list is the same as in the *Categories*. But he goes straight on to gloss this account by explaining that to say what a thing is—to give its nature—is to signify a substance or a quantity or a quality, and so on through the list. The discrepancy is twofold. The list which he gives first contains no mention of substance, while the second does; and the first list treats the nature as just one of the categories, while the second treats it as somehow transcending the categories or as subject to variation in accordance with the differences between the categories.[19]

The apparent inconsistency is so glaring that we are bound to believe that it is illusory. Aristotle's next comments indicate that he thinks so too. He starts by articulating the rationale of the second version of the list of categories. When we have something exhibited to us and try to say what it is, the answers are to be distinguished according to which one of the ten categories is being signified. Thus when we say that something is a man, we signify a substance; when we say that something is a white colour, we signify a quality, and so on. But this is followed by a passage which reminds us of the first version of the list:

> In each case, if either the thing itself or its genus is said about itself, it signifies what it is. But if it is said about something else, it signifies not what it is but a quantity or a quality or one of the other categories.(*Top.* A9, 103b35-4al).

Here we have the contrast between saying something which signifies a thing's nature, and saying things which signify its quantity and so on; and this is how we find the categories contrasted in the first version of the list presented in this passage.

The apparent inconsistency between the lists can be reconciled. The key lies in the contrast between 'saying something about itself' and 'saying something about something else'. Where something is said about itself, what is said will in all cases signify a nature but this nature will vary in accordance with the second version of the list of categories—substance, quality, and so on. Where something is said about something else, there is a contrast between what signifies the nature and what signifies one of the other categories; moreover, in this case there is no possibility that something should signify a substance.

The contrast between these two ways of 'saying something' seems to be a contrast between using terms to *identify* things and to *describe* them. Both uses belong to general predicate terms. In their identifying use, predicates exhibit categorial differences. Some identify the nature of a thing, others identify a quality or a quantity, and so on. In their descriptive use, predicates express various features which things possess, and the categories serve to distinguish these predicates. The lists of categories which result from analysing these two uses of predicates are almost identical. This is because the items which we pick out when we describe something are also capable of being directly identified. But the lists diverge over the category of substance. Predicates which signify a substance can be used to identify things, as when we say that something is a man or a table; but with these there is no distinct descriptive use. It is not possible first to identify something by a general predicate, and then to use a second predicate to describe it in such a way that the second signifies a substance.

So the distinction between identification and description provides a good explanation for the two features of *Top.* A9 which caused problems of interpretation—the omission of 'substance' from one of the lists of categories, and the divergent treatments of a thing's nature in the two lists. We can also now begin to see the real purpose of the theory and to resolve our earlier uncertainty about its status in relation to ontological and linguistic analysis. An important constraint on a successful resolution of these problems is that it should accommodate the factors which we have already canvassed in support of particular theories about the nature of the categories.

As we said before, Aristotle's term for category means 'predicate'. To understand the theory properly we must start by examining this notion. Predicates as a linguistic phenomenon impress us by their generality. Predicates differ fundamentally from names in that they do not denote a single individual. Aristotle's various accounts of the categories do not mention proper names; we should remember this in view of the temptation to present such items as Socrates and Callias as examples to illustrate the category of substance. Socrates may be an example of a substance. But this is a piece of shorthand, and it needs to be spelled out: 'a man' signifies a substance and Socrates is an example of what it signifies. This fuller way of stating the condition reflects the primary role of predicates, as opposed to names, in the theory of categories.

Let us enquire further into the philosophical rationale of this linguistic practice. We are speculating here, since Aristotle gives no reason for omitting proper names from the theory of categories. But he does occasionally indicate, in other contexts of discussion, a view that names are semantically open, that nothing in the nature of such a name carries any entailment as to the kind of thing which it names.[20] Certain commentators on Frege have developed this view in defence of his claim that predicates play an ineliminable role in any adequate theory of the meaning of proper names.[21]

It is natural to suppose that names secure and retain reference to things in the world by a process analogous to ostension. Just as we can refer to things by pointing and using the demonstrative 'that', so proper names are linguistic pointers which attach our sentences directly to items in the world. The prevailing habits of current usage lull us into this view of proper names. This usage assigns such names primarily to persons, centres of settlement, and some natural features, such as mountains and rivers. No doubt the practice reflects our valuation of the relative importance of being able to refer to these particular named items in the world which we experience. But we are not thereby compelled to assign any logically special status to them, despite our interest. We could alter our linguistic habits and assign names to any other identifiable item; and if some significant shift occurred in our focus of interest, we would probably do so.

There is the logical possibility, then, that a proper name could name something other than its actual referent; to move from this to the sceptical position that, as things are now, it might indeed name something else, is not difficult. 'Socrates' might name not a person but a temporal slice of a person, or the behavioural movements from which a person is only an inferred construction.[22] We do not need to take such scepticism seriously to see that something more is required than has so far been specified if we are to account for the referential role of proper names. What we require in addition is an indication, either explicit or contextually implicit, of the kind of thing that the name refers to. The ostension which supplies a reference for a proper name must be accompanied by a general predicate; this will indicate the kind of thing to which the name makes individual reference.

Thus we need to understand that 'Socrates' is the name of a physical object—perhaps, more precisely, of a person—rather than the name of some momentary state or some qualitative feature of the environment; and 'Belfast' is the name of a place, not of the people or buildings in that place. So a theory of meaning for proper names must recognise the indispensable role of general predicates in making possible an understanding of which things proper names refer to. From here it is an easy step to suppose that proper names can be dispensed with in favour of general predicates and demonstratives; for these will provide the resources for definite descriptions with the same extension as proper names.

To pursue this further would take us into areas of current philosophical controversy, whereas our purpose is to understand Aristotle's theory of categories. The work which derives from Frege shows how a theory of predicates can be important to a theory of language and how such a theory can serve as a basis for ontology. For if the meanings of predicates determine the reference of language, then those meanings set constraints on what can exist. It is not merely that we could not coherently describe a reality that failed to conform to the meanings of the predicates. We are entitled to draw the stronger conclusion that provided any of our language succeeds in referring to reality, that reality must be articulated in accordance with the fundamental distinctions revealed in the differences of meaning between predicates.

The Uses of the Categories

This view of the relation between language and reality enables us to understand the motivation of Aristotle's theory of categories and to account for those features which inclined us to construe it as an exercise either in ontology or in linguistic analysis. Suppose that it is sound strategy to approach ontology by attending to major and fundamental distinctions in the ways in which we talk about what there is; we would expect a theory of categories to assume the appearance of an exercise in the analysis of reality, even while it explores the linguistic differences among predicates. At the heart of the enterprise which Aristotle constructs for himself, is the unravelling of some key ambiguities. In Aristotle's view, neglect of these ambiguities was crucially responsible for the inadequate ontologies offered by Plato and the Presocratics.

The first ambiguity concerns change. When we contemplate the varieties of change, there seem to be four main kinds—change of place, change of size, change of quality and change of nature.[23] Each of these contains more specific kinds: change of temperature is a different qualitative change from change of colour, and movement upwards is a different local change from movement forwards. But the distinctions among these specific kinds are uncontroversial once we have the concept of the general kind of change under which they fall. Not so, however, with the four general kinds themselves. Here it is less easy to grasp how all these forms of change can coexist and yet be distinct from each other. In particular, one might question the distinction between change of quality and change of nature. The idea behind qualitative change is that the subject changes in respect of some property, while retaining its identity as well as its location and extent. With change of nature, on the other hand, there is a failure to retain identity (as well as location and extent). Yet how are we to identify a thing except in terms of its properties, and are we really justified in speaking of the same subject if these properties are taken on or given up? Such questions cast doubt on the distinction between these two forms of change; and analogous difficulties could be made for change of place and of size.

Aristotle draws a lesson from these problems: change is a complex concept, and our characteristic ways of talking about it are ambiguous. It is not just that change comes in many forms, requiring of the analyst no more than that he produce a taxonomy of its varieties. If things were that simple, we would not find theories which assimilated or failed to recognise the distinctness of some one or more of these four general modes—or even assimilated them. The most significant of these distortions involves a failure to recognise change of nature as a distinct mode of change; but there was also a view, maintained for example by the Atomists, that reduced all change to change of place.[24]

His solution is to deny the assumption on which such reductionist claims are based, namely that there is a single concept of change. Talk of change is elliptical unless supplemented by an indication of the category in respect of which the change is claimed to occur. This means, in accordance with what we have already learned about the theory of categories, that any particular attribution of change must be understood with reference to a general predicate. This is true even of those changes of nature or substance where ordinary language speaks of the change in absolute terms; here too something can come to be only if there is something that it comes to be.[25] The theory of categories, being a theory of predicates, will then provide a systematic means of understanding what is required for a change of the type specified by the particular predicate. It will give rules for determining whether the predicate signifies a substance or a quality; once we are clear about this, we should not be tempted to construe the change on the basis of an inappropriate model.

Thus we know from the theory of categories that qualities have opposites but substances do not. It follows that a general proposal to analyse change in terms of a succession among opposite states will not straightforwardly cover both these modes of change; and a proposal of this kind will only be of any use if it is specially adapted to fit each distinct category.[26] But we shall hold over further investigation of this matter until the fuller discussion of change in Chapter 5; our present aim is to understand the general nature and purpose of the theory of categories. In the case of change general distinctions are drawn from the theory of predicates, and these determine the conditions which must be observed in an adequate account of the changes which occur in the nature of things.

The categories are also used to resolve crucial ambiguities which come with the concept of being. The way in which Aristotle makes his point is bound up with a usage of Greek which is hard to reproduce in English. To bring out in English what I take to be his point, I shall adapt his language somewhat. Consider the open formula 'there is such a thing as F', where the values of F are general predicates.[27] The ambiguity is in the word 'thing'; what this word means depends on the category of the particular predicate. For example, if the predicate were 'singing', to claim that there is such a thing is to claim that there is such an activity. But the same analysis will not work if the predicate is 'white'; in this case 'quality', rather than 'activity', must be substituted for 'thing' in the original formula. So no single analysis will cover all occasions on which the formula is used, but the theory of categories provides a means of mounting a finite number of analyses and so of creating order where otherwise there would be anarchy.

The most important category here is substance, as with the earlier example of change. If the semantic complexity of 'thing' is not recognised, the special position of substance among the kinds of predicate almost certainly will not be understood. In that case we shall have a theory of predicates, and consequent ontological theory, which allows for no ordering of prior and posterior among the items which it considers.[28] The theorising will not just be incomplete; the material for which it does offer some analysis will actually be distorted. That is why Aristotle's diagnosis of the problem leads him to postulate ambiguities. The way to clear them up is by analysing language; only then can muddle in ontology be avoided.

Aristotle uses the theory of categories to develop difficulties in Plato's theory of Forms along lines which were first sketched by Plato in the *Parmenides*.[29] The Third Man argument, in the original form in which it occurs in that work, exploits the habit of simultaneously construing a general term in two opposed ways—as a predicate which is common to many subjects, and as the name of the general kind under which such subjects fall. The theory of Forms, against which the argument is directed, amounts to an assertion of the second view; according to this theory the reference of general predicates is a separate object. But much of the motivation for the theory is supplied by reflection on the mechanism whereby we are able to apply predicates to a plurality of subjects; thus the first view of predicates is not foreign to the spirit of the theory.

We have emphasised the interpretation of Aristotle's categories as a theory of predicates. It might be expected, therefore, that the effect of applying the theory to the Third Man argument would be to condemn interpreting predicates as any kind of name. So is this the point at issue between Aristotle and Plato?

We must see that it is not. Aristotle's theory is a theory of predicates, but it is not just any such theory. We want an interpretation which will show how this particular theory, with its analysis of predicates into ten fundamental kinds, can serve in an argument for the rejection of Plato's ontology. The answer is best indicated in the *Topics* passage considered earlier. We saw there how the distinction between substance and the other categories supports a division in the role of predicates: they can be used either to identify or to describe a subject. Substance predicates only have the former role, but predicates in other categories can perform either function.[30] If the varieties of predicates are understood in these ways, the difficulties about general terms highlighted by the Third Man argument will not arise.

It is characteristic of Plato's ontology to construe every general term as referring in the same way. This presupposition underlies the theory of Forms, with its central tenet that corresponding to each kind of thing there is a single object, and also provides a crucial premiss for the Third Man argument. Aristotle's objection is that the ways in which general terms refer are irreducibly plural; and he supports this claim with his analysis of the tenfold category division and, above all, the separation of substances from other kinds of predicate.

Platonism, with its ontological extravagance, and the niggardly nominalism opposed to it have this in common: both fail to recognise the complexity in the ways in which predicates identify things. Some predicates identify things directly, whereas others operate indirectly by picking out features of those subjects which the first kind indicate; and the other kinds of predicate can be distinguished in nine ways. Thus when I call something 'a horse', I use a predicate to identify it for what it is; but when I call it 'white' or 'standing', I identify it only indirectly, by identifying a feature of the thing rather than the thing itself. Moreover the logical differences in these two predicates, such as susceptibility to variation in degree, indicate that the features which they identify are fundamentally distinct. Platonists want to construe every predicate as directly referential, in the manner of substance predicates; nominalists reject the suggestion that non-substance predicates have reference at all. Aristotle, however, uses considerations derived from an analysis of the modes of signification of predicates, to advance a more complex and subtle view of the ontological implications of our ability to use general terms.

Aristotle and Kant

The aim in this chapter has been to review the general nature of the theory of categories and the uses to which it is put. The theory is much occupied with matters of language and, through the use of the term 'category', proclaims itself to be an analysis of linguistic items; so why does it frequently assume a more or less explicitly ontological guise? Some of Aristotle's remarks on categories might suggest that he falls victim to use/mention confusion. But he says enough to warn those who read him carefully that this charge of confusion is unlikely to stick.

Here is an example of an apparent howler which on reflection is shown to be no such thing. He compares and contrasts fallacies arising from bad grammar (such as supposing that all plural nouns are formed by adding '-s' or past tense verbs by adding '-ed') with those which depend on mistakes about the signification of an element of speech (such as supposing that 'standing' signifies an activity or 'white' a substance). He comments on the relation between these phenomena of argument: 'The result is that just as those arguments are ungrammatical with things, so these are with names; for a man and white are both a thing and a name.'[31] The assimilation of the two cases may seem at first to rest on a confusion between the use and mention of the words 'man' and 'white'. But this cannot be right, since it is also part of Aristotle's point that the two cases are different. There is undeniably a *similarity* between the use and mention of words; and provided this similarity is not interpreted as identity, the charge of confusion fails.

The correct interpretation is that Aristotle adopts a conscious strategy of deducing ontological conclusions from linguistic premisses. We have followed his argument as he mounts a Fregean attempt to base sound ontological theory on correct discrimination among the varieties of predicate and, above all, on the recognition of the primary place occupied by substance predicates in our identification of things. The resulting ontology has a bonus, of an Austinian kind, in that it does not require us to talk nonsense about what exists—something which, Aristotle believed, Plato could not avoid. But the deep reason why nonsense and falsehood should be so connected is that, broadly speaking, the world depends on how we use general predicates to identify its inhabitants.

We can now see that Aristotle's theory of categories is not so remote from Kant's as we initially suggested. To be sure, Kant's is a theory of *a priori* concepts, and neither of these epistemological notions figures in Aristotle's discussions. On the other hand, Kant reaches his particular list of concepts by analysing the logical features of judgements, in which predicates play an essential role;[32] and Kant, anticipating Frege, also recognises the general and predicative nature of concepts. So when we look at the detailed context of Kant's selection of his categories, his motivation turns out to be not so different from Aristotle's.

More significant, I believe, is the aprioricity of Kant's categories. In his theory these concepts determine the form which any reality we can understand must take. It is not that we are first presented with an independent reality which we can then go on to compare with our concepts; rather, the only way in which we can be presented with reality is through these categorial concepts. Aristotle's view of the role of his categorial predicates is essentially similar. He would not want to place any strongly idealist construction on this claim; it is, after all, *reality* which these predicates enable us to grasp. But without them, there is no reality, and without the analysis of language, no possibility of ontology.

Notes

1 G. Ryle, *The Concept of Mind* (London, 1949), pp.16-18; cf. also 'Categories', in *Collected Papers*, vol.2 (London, 1971), esp. p.174.

2 *Critique of Pure Reason* A79-81/B105-7.

3 M.A.E. Dummett, 'Can analytical philosophy be systematic, and ought it to be?', repr. in *Truth and Other Enigmas* (London, 1978), pp.437-58.

4 J.L. Ackrill, *Aristotle's Categories and De Interpretatione* (Oxford, 1963), pp.80, 107. M. Frede, who also recognises the importance of the *Topics* passage, argues for 'predication' rather than 'predicate', in 'Categories in Aristotle' in D.J. O'Meara (ed.), *Studies in Aristotle* (Washington, 1981), pp.1-24; but he allows that the distinction is a fine one (p.8), and in any case the point does not affect our present discussion.

5 The closest Greek comes is with the use of the definite article in combination with another word which would be grammatically impossible if the word were being used rather than mentioned; cf. e.g. *S.E.*14, 173b28, 38. From this usage one can readily extend this analysis to cases where the combination is not grammatically impossible, but caution is always necessary; for some salutary remarks, see G.E.L. Owen, 'Dialectic and Eristic in the Treatment of the Forms', in his (ed.) *Aristotle On Dialectic* (Oxford, 1968), p.115.

6 *Cat.* 5, 2a34-b6.

7 *Cat.* 5, 2a11-19.

8 *Cat.* 2; 5, 2a19-34. G.E.L. Owen, 'The Platonism of Aristotle', *Proceedings of the British Academy* 51 (1965), pp.133-9, argues that the distinction is inspired by reflection on the Third Man problem in Plato's theory of Forms.

9 For variation in degree, see *Cat.* 5, 3b33-4a9; 6,6a19-25; 7, 6b19-27; 8, 10b26-11a14, where the significance of the criterion is carefully explored.

10 *Cat.* 7, 6a36-b2; cf. *S.E.* 31, 181b26-8. The origins of the criterion can be seen in Plato *Symposium* 199d-e, *Republic* 438a7-b5.

11 *Cat.* 7, 8a28-b21; cf. *Top.* Z4, 142a28-31.

12 Chapter 1 pp.17-18 above.

13 For example, *Top.* Δ1, 120b36-1a9; cf. H1, 152a38-9.

14 Other passages in *S.E.* which use the idea of category confusion are 4, 166b10-19; 6, 168a25-6; 7, 169a29-36.

15 This interpretation is confirmed by Aristotle's comparison, at *S.E.* 14, 174a5-9, between gross grammatical solecisms and the kind of faulty argument we are considering here. To think that e.g. all English verbs ending in '-ed' are past tense (contrast 'fled' and 'shed') is to make, at the most superficial level, the grammatical mistake made by one who thinks that all verbs not preceded by 'be' are active. See below, p.57.

16 Some prepositions are included in his analysis of philosophically significant examples of multiple meaning—'according to' (*Met.* Δ18), 'out of ' (*Met.* Δ24); cf. *Phys.* Δ3, 210a25-33 on 'in'.

17 *Cat.* 8, 10a27-32. Sometimes grammatical differences are significant for the theory of categories (cf. *Cat.* 7, 6b11-14); but this requires separate justification.

18 Ackrill, pp.79-80, and Frede (see n.4 of this chapter) comment on the *Topics* passage. Otherwise the neglect persists, despite Ackrill's complaint.

19 All this occurs within the eight lines of *Top*. A9, 103b21-9. None of the terminology in this presentation is out of line with Aristotle's normal usage.

20 At *Met*. Z4, 1030a7-9 (cf. *An. Post*. B7, 92b30-2) Aristotle objects to the idea that extensional equivalence between a descriptive formula and a proper name can make the description into a definition; otherwise the verses that make up the poem of the *Iliad* would be a definition. What underlies this objection is the thought that the name '*Iliad*' lacks intrinsic semantic content.

21 See M.A.E. Dummett, *Frege: Philosophy of Language* (London, 1981), pp.94-9. C.M.G. Wright, *Frege's Conception of Numbers as Objects* (Aberdeen, 1983), pp.43-4.

22 This line of thought is developed by S. Kripke, *Wittgenstein on Rules and Private Language* (Blackwell, 1982), pp.13-21. He acknowledges its anticipation in N. Goodman, *Fact, Fiction, and Forecast* (London, 1954), pp.74-80.

23 *Phys*. Γ1, 200b32-1a9; E1, 225b5-9.

24 *G.C.* A8, 325a23-34; *Cael*. Γ4, 303a4-12.

25 This is most thoroughly argued in *G.C.* A3, 318a27-19a22, where it is shown that the ordinary language distinction between 'become' and 'become F' does not infringe the principle that some predicate enters into the analysis of every kind of change, including apparently absolute ones.

26 *Phys*. A5, 188b21-6; A6, 189a32-b3. Cf. S. Waterlow, *Nature, Change, and Agency in Aristotle's Physics* (Oxford, 1982), pp.9-14.

27 My adaptation is suggested by *Met*. Δ7, 1017a22-30, where Aristotle harnesses the categories to the analysis of 'exist'. 'Thing' in my formula is intended to indicate the role that predicates can play in existential analysis. Some light is shed on this difficult issue by G.E.L. Owen, 'Aristotle on the Snares of Ontology', in R. Bambrough (ed.), *New Essays on Plato and Aristotle* (London, 1962), pp.69-95, esp. 84-7.

28 Here one might mention the logical or conceptual priority of substance over the other categories (*Met*. Γ2, 1003a33-b10; Z1, 1028a10-20, a34-6) which plays so important a role in Aristotle's characterisation of the nature of ontology; cf. G.E.L. Owen, 'Logic and metaphysics in some earlier works of Aristotle', in I. Düring and G.E.L. Owen (eds.), *Aristotle and Plato in the Mid-Fourth Century* (Göteborg, 1960), pp.163-90, and my comments in *Aristotle's Concept of Dialectic* (Cambridge, 1977), pp.41-9. But the theory of focal meaning in turn depends on the argument about predication in *Top*. A9, discussed below.

29 For references to the texts in Plato and Aristotle, see Chapter 1, n.18 above.

30 *Top*. A9, 103b35-9.

31 *S.E.* 14, 174a7-9.

32 *Critique of Pure Reason* A68-9/B93-4.

CHAPTER 4

Ontology

The theory of categories is an exercise in the philosophy of language rather than in ontology, but it does set constraints on any permissible ontology. In particular it excludes what we may call *monochrome* ontologies—those that use a uniform pattern to construe the existence of whatever they claim does exist. Such an ontology might recognise as equally real all those items that are successfully referred to by general predicates, or again it might restrict reality so that predicates could occur in true sentences and yet have no reference. An example of the first sort is Plato's theory of Forms, which associates reality (a Form) with each general predicate; the other approach is found in ancient Greek atomic theory, in which the only predicates which have reference are those attributing shape, position and order.[1]

The theory of categories reveals the complexity of the notion of existing or being a thing. Both the spendthrift Plato and the skinflint Atomist fail to see this. Moreover the theory provides a further condition for an adequate ontology: it must reflect the primacy of substance. We can understand what it is for anything other than a substance to exist only if we understand its relation of dependence on a substance; for the sense of the claim that there exists such a thing as F, where 'F' signifies something non-substantial, is brought out by an analysis which explicitly mentions that substances are F.

This is why Aristotle can replace the old question, 'what is there?' by the more definite and refined question, 'what is substance?'.[2] The proposal to reduce the one question to the other is a good indication of the importance of the theory of categories for ontology. But much in ontology is left unresolved, even after that proposal; and there is much to be done before an answer can be found to our more refined question. This is the topic of the notoriously difficult investigation which occupies *Metaphysics* Z.[3]

Substance

The question 'what is substance?' can have an extensional or an intensional interpretation, and Aristotle does not distinguish them at all sharply. He asks which things actually are substances; and he extends the enquiry to some controversial candidates, such as numbers and Platonic Forms. He also asks what is it that makes a substance to be a substance—in what does its substancehood consist. This question leads to an examination of the relative importance of the matter and the form of substances. The two approaches interact; for considerations bearing on the intension of the notion of substance serve to enlarge or to retract its extension, and certain paradigmatic items in the extension, such as individual living creatures, exert control over the plausibility of candidates for the intension. When Aristotle scrutinises universals, where the question is both whether there are such substances and whether a universal is what makes each substance to be what it is, the extensional and intensional approaches become indistinguishable.[4]

The ontological discussion we shall consider is a very complex structure built round a starkly simple problem. If we take some paradigm substance, such as a particular man, we can distinguish two aspects of it. There is the physical stuff of which it consists—the limbs, tissues and chemicals which make up an organic body; and there is the general kind which this individual, as a whole entity, instantiates. Both the matter and the universal kind may be seen as essential to the existence of this particular thing. Without the matter we would not be able to distinguish it from other things of the same kind, and without the universal we could not grasp what it is that we are thus distinguishing. It is not simply that such an individual man needs both to be constituted out of matter and to belong to a universal kind in order to be what he is. This substance needs each of these in order to be the *particular individual* that it is.

So there is a strong *prima facie* case for answering our original question, 'what is substance?' with both 'matter' and 'the universal'. This plunges us immediately into a difficulty. Matter and universals seem to be as opposed as any two ontological items can be.[5] Matter particularises; it fulfils precisely the function of separating one thing off from another. Universals generalise; they collect together the individuals which matter distinguishes. What a universal does, matter undoes; and vice versa.

It is natural to suppose that we have here not one but two insights into the nature of substance, and that they are incompatible. The situation would be dialectically similar to one in which the answer to a question about the goal in life was 'a good life and one which appears good to him who chooses it'. But we learned in Chapter 2 that an account which combines apparent opposites is fatally premature. A proper insight can be reached only by developing each of the opposing views and then moving to deal with the contradiction between them. There is no easier or quicker way to a satisfactory resolution.

That is how we should proceed with the problem of substance. Aristotle first develops the case for claiming that matter is substance, and then he finds an insuperable difficulty in it. Next he proceeds in a similar way with the claim that a universal is substance; and this too is beset by unacceptable consequences. By the time we have appreciated how these difficulties arise from each suggestion it should be clear not only that the accounts are inadequate but why they are. The way will have been prepared for a third account which combines the merits of the first two but does not generate objections in the way that they do. The key to this resolution will be a grasp of how the first two accounts, despite appearances to the contrary, do not in fact conflict.

Matter

We start with the view that the matter of an individual thing is its substance or, more generally, that matter is substance. It is natural for us today to construe the term 'substance' in this way, influenced as we are by the corpuscular theory of the seventeenth century and the ontologies which philosophers developed out of it.[6] It comes more easily to us to speak of the substance of a table, meaning the wood or iron of which it is made, than of the table as a substance. Such things as salt and cement are counted as substances more readily than the complex structured items of which they are ingredients. Although the association between stuff and substance was less commonly made in Aristotle's time, he too was aware of such theories, a notable example being the theory of Anaxagoras.[7] But in any case he provides an argument for the identification.

In order to appreciate this argument, it is helpful to know something of Aristotle's biological and chemical theories. The argument will depend not on the truth of these particular theories, but only on the assumption that some theory of matter along these general lines is true. But Aristotle's particular theory provides a good illustration of the general approach, and it will be helpful to work with it. If we start with a paradigm substance, such as a living creature, its matter can be analysed at four levels. In the first place there is the entire physical organism, which is the material component of a creature capable of performing life functions. This is itself a structure of constituent parts, such as face, hands and heart; and so, at the second level of analysis, these things should be regarded as the matter out of which the whole organism is structured. We reach a third level when we see that these material components are themselves structures composed of simpler material stuffs such as blood and flesh. Aristotle calls these the uniform parts, by contrast with the non-uniform parts at the second level; and it is proper to regard them as the matter of the non-uniform parts. The application of this line of thought leads to a fourth level. The uniform parts—blood and flesh—can themselves be analysed into more elementary constituents. Such things are structured ratios of elemental stuffs—in fact, the four traditional elements, fire, air, water and earth.[8] So for the same reason that we regard the elements as the matter of the uniform parts, we should also see these parts as the matter of the more complex items which they in turn make up.

By this analysis we reach the following hierarchy, this time working from the bottom up: elements, uniform parts, non-uniform parts, complete organisms. In every case the earlier item is the matter for the next one in the list. Now it is the mark of substance, unlike things in other categories, to be a subject of attributes. If we can say in the case of something, such as a colour or a number, that something else possesses that thing, the substance is the possessor, and what it possesses is not a substance. But if we consider the relation between the material constituents of a thing and its structure and organisation (form), at any of the levels of analysis we have just distinguished, it seems that the matter is the subject and the form is an attribute which it possesses.[9]

In the case of a living organism it is the physical body which seems the best candidate for substancehood; and the verdict will go in favour of matter at whichever level of biological or chemical analysis we choose to focus attention. The general principle is this: wherever it is possible to assign a definite characterisation to a thing, there is reason to construe this as the attribute of some other thing which is its subject.[10] It is not unlike an idea employed in the translation of English into the language of the first-order predicate calculus; any general term with semantic content is represented by a predicate letter and is excluded from the domain of quantification.

The principle gains support from the kind of analysis of levels of organisation in living creatures which we explored earlier. This analysis shows how we can move from the thesis, established in the theory of categories, that substances are subjects of attributes, to the conclusion that matter is substance because its logical role is to stand as subject to the attributes of structure and form. The argument seems, then, to work to the following conclusion:

> Those who consider things in this way must see matter as the only substance. By 'matter' I mean that which in itself is said to be neither a thing nor a quantity nor anything else by which what there is is defined. For there is something of which each of these is predicated and the existence of which is different from that of each of the kinds of predicate since the rest are predicated of substance and this is predicated of matter. So what is ultimate is in itself neither a thing nor a quantity nor anything else. (*Met*. Z3, 1029a18-25)

We thus reach the idea of an ultimate subject. This idea seems essential to our notion of matter; so matter must be substance if it is a criterion of substance that it should be a logical subject.

Having developed the analysis of matter to this conclusion, Aristotle observes immediately that it is unacceptable.[11] Such a subject will lack separate and individual existence, which it must have if it is to be substance. Independent existence is absolutely basic to the conception of the priority of substance among the categories. The predicates in this category serve to identify distinct individuals; and that is why substance is the first category. Any further account of substance which subverts this insight must be faulty. But this is the very test that the account of matter as substance fails. In order to sustain the claim that some thing is a distinct individual, one needs a predicate to mark it off from the background of features with which it partially overlaps. One needs to understand the thing *as a man*, for example. Sortal predicates in the category of substance achieve this result; even mass predicates would serve the purpose, whether these be understood as designating the whole amount of some stuff or any lesser quantity of it. Blood, whether construed as a totality or counted body by body, is still a definite subject and as such can be distinguished from other things.

If every means which we have for definitely characterising a thing is analysed as a feature to be distinguished from the subject which possesses it, and if the only substance is a featureless matter, then it turns out that we lack the means for distinguishing the material subject from any of its (alleged) features. We end up not with an ultimate subject but with a thing that is in principle excluded from being a subject.

This is Aristotle's argument against the claim that matter is substance. It seems to make a telling point; but on closer inspection it is hard to focus on it precisely. What exactly is Aristotle's target here? Is he attacking the general claim that matter is substance, or is he refuting a more specialised thesis that totally characterless matter—what is sometimes called 'prime matter'—is substance?

We shall examine these two possibilities, starting with the second. It seems the natural way to construe the result of Aristotle's progressive analysis of matter. Each later step in this analysis shows that the method used to characterise the preceding step revealed something that is a feature possessed by matter rather than matter itself. So it is natural to suppose that we have not really reached matter at all until we have stripped away all such features. The featureless bare substratum, prime matter, is the only genuine matter.

The difficulty with this argument is that if the counter-considerations brought by Aristotle are strong enough to defeat it, they also tell against this particular interpretation of his target. Suppose that it is incoherent to try to distinguish a pure subject from all the features which characterise it. Then the theorist promoting such a conception of prime matter is a victim of muddle; but so also is a philosophical critic who offers this as an interpretation of what the theorist is trying to do.[12] Whatever the precise view is that Aristotle is rejecting, the reasons he gives rule out that *this* should be the view.

The interpretation has another drawback; it leaves intact the general thesis that matter is substance. Some matter—namely, prime matter—would indeed be disqualified. But not all matter is prime; in particular, there would be left the relatively organised varieties of matter which we considered earlier—the elements, the uniform parts of organisms, their non-uniform parts, and the whole organisms themselves. These do not obviously lack the separate and individual existence which Aristotle denies to a bare subject. So the thesis which he professes to be examining would still stand. We would not be able to rule out the claim that matter is substance.

We must, therefore, examine the alternative interpretation; here Aristotle's target will be matter in general. This is immediately supported by all the considerations which we have marshalled against the first interpretation. There is sound reason to think that the notion of prime matter is too incoherent to be the target of Aristotle's argument; and it is natural to suppose that we have somehow misinterpreted the development of the case for matter as substance. Whatever that case amounts to, it cannot issue in the conception of matter as an utterly pure and featureless subject. So an attack on the claim that matter is substance must be directed against a more determinate kind of matter.

The second interpretation of Aristotle's intention in *Met.* Z3 derives strong support from this argument. But here too there is a major difficulty. One theme recurs throughout the entire investigation of substance; any attempt to abstract the material component from our understanding of a substance produces an intolerable distortion. Immaterial substances tend to contradict their own nature: a man without matter is not a man. If to reject the claim that matter is substance is to exclude a thing's matter from the notion of that thing as a substance, then something essential to that substance is removed.

Here is something that is unquestionably a substance—the man Socrates. Aristotle notes that to construe such a substance in a way that abstracts the person from the material that is his body, is to fail to capture its nature. Some Platonists had supposed that just as geometry should pay no attention to materials like wood or bronze, even though in the natural world circles and squares are realised in such material media, so also there can be an idealised biology that ignores physical bodies.[13] The patent absurdity of this idea demonstrates the essential role of matter in the conception of natural substances. But if bodily matter is essential to the separate and individual existence of the substance Socrates, it seems impossible that Aristotle's strictures on matter in *Met.* Z3 should be directed against this kind of matter. So they do not touch the claim that all matter is substance, which is how we are construing the target of Aristotle's attack according to this interpretation.

Each interpretation appears to give rise to difficulties. Final comment must await analysis of the other main contender for the title of substance—the universal. But we can indicate a further interpretation which combines what is attractive in each of the first two. Any conception of matter which makes it natural to extend the analysis of matter down to the ultimate substratum, prime matter, must be inadequate. We have seen what lent credibility to a conception of this kind; it was the idea that the bearer of formal or structural features could be identified independently of them. So it was easy to suppose, for example, that the blood and flesh that can be organised into the structure of a hand, can be picked out independently of this structure. If we believe this to be possible, we are committed to the view that things can be identified without reference to their structure; and this leads inevitably to the incoherent notion of prime matter.

Yet Aristotle cannot accept an analysis that allows this incoherence to damage the whole notion of matter. We avoid this result by adjusting the idea of matter so as to block the route to prime matter. Rather than identifying the matter of a thing independently from the thing itself, we should instead try to abstract the matter by inspecting the structure into which it is organised. To illustrate this contrast, consider an eye. The wrong approach is to suppose that we can identify the jelly and fluids that are its matter, and subsequently examine how they are structured to make up an eye. The correct method is to discover directly from the structured object itself what materials constitute it. The most effective way of doing this is to explore its potential for change.[14]

Once we have distinguished these two ways of understanding the relation between matter and what it constitutes, it is clear that it was wrong to suppose that it was necessary to choose between the two interpretations of the rebuttal of matter in Z3. It seemed that while prime matter could not be separately identified, less ultimate matter could be; and so the attack on the incoherence of prime matter did not serve also as a refutation of the more general thesis that matter is substance. What is now apparent is that the whole strategy of attempting a separate identification of matter is a mistake, at whatever level of matter the strategy is applied. Another way to see this is to reflect on how naturally the idea of prime matter arose from adopting the wrong approach to matter in general.

Universals

We must now inspect the credentials of the other leading contender for the title of substance. This is the universal; and its main claim to be taken seriously arises directly from the discussion of matter. The case for matter was based on the idea that where we can distinguish subject and predicate elements in the representation of some state of affairs, it is the subject rather than the predicate which designates the substance. If the case for matter has been shown to fail, it is natural to reverse the idea about the role of the subject and predicate elements in sentences, and to see the predicate as designating the substance. The new construction is consistent with the main insight which led to the rejection of matter as substance; this was based on the unavailability of any definite feature to individuate a pure subject. So it is reasonable to conclude that the deficiency will be made good by invoking such features as are signified by predicate terms.

Predicates are general. They can be applied to any number of things; in this way they differ quite fundamentally from proper names and definite descriptions. They seem to belong to a distinct semantic category; and when we ask what can be the basis for this difference in meaning, we find an appropriate candidate in the ontological cupboard. Universals have found friends for a number of reasons; Plato favoured them because they provided units of meaning to correspond to general predicates. So if it is predicates that succeed in referring to substances, the substances must be universals.[15] Indeed we found that matter cannot suffice to separate and distinguish individual substances precisely because it lacks the definite features which are signified by general predicates.

Consider what it is that makes two men two distinct substances. Aristotle sometimes suggests that it is their matter; each man is made up of a different quantity of matter.[16] But as we have seen, this does not explain the difference adequately, since these quantities of matter cannot be characterised so that each makes a distinct substance. What makes each of these quantities of matter a distinct substance is that each is a man. Appeal to the general predicate provides the means for counting the distinct items. But the predicate is general. It is true of each individual man; and it represents something that is common to both the men.[17] If we distinguish this common element from those things which it is common to, calling it a universal, then a universal is the substance of the individuals; or more briefly, a universal is a substance.

Here we have a well-attested line of thought about substance which is also a natural response to the rejection of matter. Aristotle's dialectical strategy demands that he should subject it to thorough examination; and this he does in *Met.* Z13-16. The analysis is subtle and sinuous, but its two main elements are easily discerned: first, a direct development of and attack on the idea that any universal could be a substance and, second, a less direct exploration of the idea that every universal as such is a substance. In the second phase Aristotle extends his examination to more generic universals; he is concerned to chart the relations among them, and between them and the more specific universals. His complex strategy fairly reflects the details of the investigations by philosophers, notably Plato, who had earlier worked on the theory of universals. It also sets the terms for Aristotle's own dialectical refutation of the claim that universals—any universals—are substances.

One major issue should be mentioned now, to be taken up later in detail. On the one hand, all universals are to be treated equally in the examination of the claim that universals are substances. Genera, such as Animal—or even Substance— are covered as much as species, such as Man and Horse. On the other hand, it can be argued that we must recognise a fundamental difference between specific and more generic universals. To take this line is to leave open which kind of universal is to serve as flagship of the claim that universals are substances.[18]

We shall return to this distinction. But first let us review the main arguments which Aristotle brings against the general claim that universals are substances. There are four of them. First, he emphasises that a universal is common to a number of distinct things. If these are substances, then the universal belongs to distinct substances; if they are not substances, we lose a motive for construing the universal as a substance. So we are only concerned with the first possibility. Against the universalist's analysis of this it is sufficient to point out that the substances are distinct. Their substancehood cannot derive from something common to both, which the universal is. Universals and individuals are utterly opposed, and it is not possible to explain either the individuality of things by appeal to universals or the universality of things by appeal to individuals.[19]

In the second argument Aristotle explores the supposition that universals provide the substance of those substances which fall under them, and objects that this infringes the principle that one substance cannot contain another. The principle plays an important role in the whole discussion of substance. It supports the idea of the separate and distinct existence of each substance, already mentioned in our comments on matter. If each substance is to be a genuinely single thing, it cannot be a plurality of things. But if it were to consist of a number of actually existing substantial universals, this is just what it would be.[20]

This second objection depends on our supposing that a substance can fall under more than one universal; and so it will if we include among the universal substances a subject's genus and differentia, not to mention their genera and differentiae. This leads to Aristotle's third argument, which anticipates an embarrassment that Berkeley was to press upon Locke.[21] If a generic universal is a substance, it must be subject to the principle of non-contradiction. It cannot both have and not have some attribute: either it has it or it does not. So the universal substance Animal will be either two-footed or not two-footed. The problem is that to deny either of these disjuncts is unacceptable if we consider *an animal* as a substance. For there are some animals which are two-footed and also some which are four-footed, and if four-footed, not two-footed. So, to speak generally, an animal is both two-footed and not two-footed. The generic universal *an animal* is what we refer to when we speak generally about animals, if we are to take seriously the claim that universals are substances. This substance, then, will exhibit the contradictory attributes of being two-footed and also not two-footed.[22]

An analysis of this kind can easily be carried out with almost any predicate that can be applied to more than one kind of thing. Here we uncover a problem that lies deep in the enterprise of explaining things by reference to universal substances. The general form of the problem is this: for universals to fulfil their primary function, which is to enable us to understand the relations between the general kinds into which things fall, they must be connected in ways that make it impossible to treat them as subjects of predication. We cannot enquire into the attributes of the genus Animal if we are to keep that genus serviceable for the purposes of definition; for if it has any attributes, they must make their subject self-contradictory.[23]

So from a proper appreciation of the role of universals in definition, it follows that they cannot be substances. Aristotle is at his closest point of contact here with Frege. In Frege's theory what a predicate—any predicate—refers to is precisely *not* an object.[24] Aristotle is led to examine universals in Met. Z because there seems reason to believe that predicates refer to substances; and for him substances are the primary kind of object.

The third argument against the thesis that universals are substances demonstrates that by overemphasising predicates we arrive at an unacceptable view of what they designate. What they designate are universals. But since predicates designate no object, universals cannot be the objects designated by predicates. Therefore universals are not objects, and so not substances. The argument strikes at the heart of this whole phase of Aristotle's investigation of substance—the examination of universals. If it succeeds, the analysis of predicates cannot provide the key to the nature of substance.

The fourth argument against universals continues to press the idea that the mark of predicates is their generality. The more general the predicate, the more effectively it demonstrates what predicates tell us about the nature of a substance. Let us take the substance Socrates and ask what kind of thing he is. Since we are interested in *kinds*, which are necessarily general, we shall pursue the enquiry to its most general limit. Which of Socrates' attributes links him with the largest number of other substances? The question will be satisfactorily answered by any attribute that connects him with all other substances. Candidates for such attributes are: one, a thing, a substance. Socrates is each of these. It is hard to imagine that a more general kind could be found in which to locate him. Might not one of these universals be the substance of what Socrates is?[25]

The trouble with this approach is that it is too indirect. To be sure, Socrates is one substantial thing. But this is an immediate fact about Socrates himself, not something that is only mediated by a long sequence of relations between Socrates and various universals under which he falls. Socrates is a man immediately, because this is the species to which he primarily belongs. He is mediately an animal, because he belongs in this genus by virtue of his membership of the species Man. So if Substance, One and Thing are the most universal kinds under which he falls, he does so only mediately and in virtue of the more specialised universals which define him more precisely. But this is the wrong way round. Only if Socrates is one substantial thing, is it in principle possible for him to be a man or an animal.

As with the discussion of matter, critical opinion is divided over just which thesis about universals gets rejected through these arguments. There are two possibilities: either all universals, from the most specific to the most general, are the target, or the thesis under attack is the more restricted one that universals which are predicated of other universals are substances. Why should we contemplate this restriction? It is necessary to examine the term 'universal' more closely. This is a coinage of Aristotle's. It is shorthand for a fuller expression which he sometimes uses in these chapters: 'what is said of something as a whole'.[26] The extended version makes it clear that a universal is essentially what is signified by a predicate and, more importantly, that the subject of such a predicate is itself something general—a whole. Every man is an animal, meaning that animal is said of man as a whole; and what is universal here is not only the predicate but also the subject, 'man', since the predicate is said of this universally.

By contrast, where the predicate signifies a most specific kind, such as man, it will not be possible to predicate it universally, because there will be no general term to slot into the gap in the schema 'every__is a G'. This provides a ground for distinguishing specific from more general universals; it might be, then, that Aristotle's target in this section of his examination of substance is the more specialised thesis that non-specific universals are substances.

Moreover, two of the four arguments against universals considered above depend on the assumption that generic universals are substances. The presence of these two in the critique supports the suggestion that Aristotle is adopting this more precise focus. But the other two arguments tell in the opposite direction. The objections which they raise against universals do not discriminate between specific and generic ones. For example, a specific universal, such as man, is common to a number of individual substances, in the same way that the generic universal animal is. The second argument does indeed depend on according full recognition to the importance of generic universals; for its basis is the premiss that each individual substance is composed of a number of universals, which would not be possible if the specific universal were taken to constitute the whole substance of such an individual. But while this approach gives full status to the genus, it does nothing to lessen the significance of the species. The second argument counts against any interpretation which would construe this section of the discussion as addressed exclusively to universals more general than the species.

Clearly there are grounds for favouring the thesis that Aristotle's target is generic universals. Any final interpretation will have to allow for this. But these grounds are not conclusive. The terms of the attack make it imperative to include specific universals in the target area. As with the discussion of matter, we have a tension between two interpretations; and the most satisfactory resolution is likely to come from seeing that the distinction between them is based on a misunderstanding of what it is to be a universal.

Form

The claims of matter and the universal are subjected to intricate examinations which appear to yield no positive conclusion. Then in the final chapter of *Met.* Z Aristotle gives a brisk and definite answer to his question. Substance is what causes a thing's matter to be that thing.[27] This account is sometimes glossed by saying that *form* is substance. But although part of the role of form is to structure and organise matter, Aristotle does not speak explicitly of form in this chapter;[28] and we shall have to explain this omission.

He illustrates his account of substance by the parallel case of syllable. He is thinking of spoken, not written language; and to bring out his point, I shall vary the example slightly.[29] The syllable BAT consists of the letters B,A,T. But while these are the only letters in it, the syllable is more than just the total of its constituent letters. The difference between BAT and TAB is enough to make this clear. To get a syllable out of these letters, they must be assembled in a certain order. Different orders produce different syllables; and not all orders will do, as we can see from such cases as TBA or ATB. The syllable is not simply the set of letters. There is something different in kind from the letters which organises them into the syllable.[30]

Let us apply this lesson to physical substances. Here too we have 'letters', the material constituents of substances; and they are structured and organised to make up discrete objects. Is the factor responsible for the structure a further material constituent itself? Aristotle argues that the parallel case of the syllable shows that the answer is no. That case reveals that the letters cannot produce a syllable without something extra which is not itself a letter. For there are no more letters than B, A and T, and so the extra item is not a letter.

Similarly, what is needed to produce a structured object out of material constituents is not some more matter but something of a different sort. If the extra item were also matter, the same problem as with letters would arise: how to achieve the structuring of the 'syllable' that is the whole physical object.

But does this new account succeed where the other two failed? It seems not. We are still faced with the fundamental question of whether this organising principle is something general or if it is peculiar to each particular syllable.[31] If the former, we shall locate substance in a universal—the structure which links every instance of BAT. If the latter, it is attached to the particular sounds that constitute a unique utterance of these letters. Aristotle can be charged with sliding over the type/token ambiguity in his letters and syllable example. The example can be interpreted in two different ways: either we are to consider the general type of syllable BAT and determine what distinguishes it from other syllable types, or it is the identity of a particular token of the syllable which is at issue. In the case of physical substances, what differentiates one general kind from another—say, a man from a horse— will be a question of structure; but what separates individual members within such kinds is the material parts from which each is made.

The analogy with letters and syllables demonstrates that, despite its perennial tendency to arise in ontology, this problem is illusory. Types and tokens of syllables there may be; but any utterance of a syllable will be a token, although such tokens do indeed fall under types. By focusing on utterances we underline the importance of actuality in this context. Why is it possible for the letters only to be uttered in certain syllabic combinations—BAT and TAB but not TBA or ATB? The structure is not an extra letter. It must be something in the letters themselves that makes certain orderings possible and rules others out. It is here that the written language gives a misleading picture of the elements that make it up. Orderings which present no problem in the written language have nothing corresponding to them in speech. Since the writing is intended to represent speech, in these cases it must in fact be misrepresenting it. The consonants have to be juxtaposed with vowels, in ways spelled out in detail in the study of phonetics, in order to be uttered at all. Only in the larger context of a syllable can the consonants actually exist.

Actuality is a mark of the particular rather than the general, of the token rather than the type. A particular syllable exists because of the way the letters are ordered. But although the syllable is particular, this is not because its letters, considered alone, are particular, nor because their order is. Both these items are abstractions from anything that actually exists. They are, moreover, abstractions of rather different sorts. The letters serve to distinguish the different tokens of the same syllable type; the way they are ordered defines the syllable type itself. These distinctions are needed in the analysis of what it is for a syllable actually to exist. But the items thus distinguished, necessarily general though they be, cannot actually exist apart from the particular token syllable.[32]

As it is with letters and syllables, so also with material substances, their parts and their kinds. The parts individuate one token from another; but this is possible only if there is some further thing to establish the required type. This further thing is the universal kind.

We are now better placed to understand why the earlier stages of our discussion were beset by uncertainties of interpretation. When Aristotle attacked the claim of matter, was his target prime matter or matter in some more structured form? We can see now that this is a false antithesis. Matter cannot actually exist in abstraction from form; and this is so because of the true nature of matter. The notion of utterly featureless matter is indeed untenable; but so equally is any constrast between this and some relatively more structured matter. The mistake made by every version of materialism is to suppose it possible to characterise matter, whether in a more or a less structured state, apart from its form. Once this characterisation has been made, there is likely to be a problem in knowing how to make sense of the matter which has been abstracted in this way. But the letters/syllable analogy indicates that any such attempt to abstract produces a distorted characterisation. The letters cannot be pronounced outside the syllable as they are pronounced within it.

The other problem of interpretation concerned the kind of

universal which Aristotle rejects as a candidate for substance: whether species are included or excluded. We noted that we would have to explain why he does not say straight out that form is substance. Universals perform an essential role in the construction of a hierarchical classificatory system; and this is what causes the difficulty. Such a system is designed to mark real similarities and differences among things; its purpose is well served by the abstractionist fiction that higher and lower genera and species are distinct entities.[33]

Useful though the system is, we know that it does rest on a fiction—indeed, a double fiction. Aristotle's arguments against universals as substances rule out the possibility that *all* universals could be substances. As we have seen, there are specific obstacles to the view that universals corresponding to *general* kinds should be substances. Species do not fail so easily, since they do not form part of the analysis of any other universal. At first this might seem to support an ontology of universals which discriminates in favour of species and against genera; but on reflection this cannot be right. Species and genus are complementary notions. They belong together in the enterprise of classification. An anti-Platonism which limits itself to non-species universals is untenable. To this extent Aristotle's arguments exclude the possibility that *any* universal is a substance.

Yet there is a crucial difference between species and other universals. The identification of separate individuals depends primarily on one of the general predicates associated with a species.[34] Aristotle deployed this insight against the materialist interpretation of substance. But 'form' and 'species' are merely two English terms for the one Aristotelian notion.[35] Unless he is guilty of gross equivocation, everything he says about the significance of form will carry implications for the correct ontological interpretation of species.

The form is the essential element in a substance's individuality; without the form the substance could not be the particular thing it is. It is quite wrong to follow Plato in regarding form as something distinct from each individual which bears it. At the same time form, as species, has a role in the system of universal classification. But its ontological status is very different from that of the more general kinds which are also found in such a system. To suppose otherwise is the fundamental misconception which Aristotle's critique of universals exposes.

The discussion which we have reviewed is complex and ambitious. Two large contrasts dominate its details—those between general and particular and between stuff and structure. Aristotle's method in handling each is thoroughly dialectical. The analysis of each member of the two dichotomies is developed to show how an attitude favouring one or other candidate only distorts the contribution which it can make to an adequate understanding of the issues. We have noted two particular errors—the belief that matter is identifiable in an unstructured state, and that species and genera are on a par ontologically.

The most striking feature of Aristotle's whole approach in ontology is the way in which the two main contrasts are worked together. The problem posed by the contrast between stuff and structure is given point by the role which each plays in individuation. On the other side, the issue of the relation between the general and the particular turns on understanding how the existence of structure makes it possible for material stuff to be actually realised. Form is the key to both problems. By focusing on this notion Aristotle takes up themes which were a leading concern both for Plato and for the Presocratics; and the manner of his response to their difficulties is of continuing interest in the pursuit of ontological questions.

Notes

1 Cf. *Met*. Γ5, 1009b11-12, and the testimonies collected by G.S. Kirk, J.E. Raven and M. Schofield (eds.), *The Presocratic Philosophers* (Cambridge, 1983), pp.409-12: only certain predicates refer to real features of the world.

2 *Met*. Z1, 1028b2-7.

3 The text bristles with difficulties: I shall discuss some, but about others I shall have to be dogmatic. For an extremely full discussion (but rarely any resolution) of virtually every difficulty, see M. Burnyeat (ed.), *Notes on Aristotle's Metaphysics Zeta* (Oxford, 1979).

4 Aristotle should not be accused of confusing the approaches; elsewhere he is perfectly able to distinguish them, cf. *Met*. I1, 1052b1-3. We should suppose that he has a purpose in not doing so in the present context.

5 The question is first posed in *Met*. B1, 995b27-9, and expanded in B3. *Met*. Z3, 1028b33-36 (cf. Z13, 1038b2-3) takes up the antithesis, and it remains in play in Z16.

6 For this contrast see J. Bennett, *Kant's Analytic* (Cambridge, 1966), pp.182-3. It corresponds to Locke's distinction between the ideas of substance in general and of the sorts of substances, cf. *An Essay Concerning Human Understanding* II.xxiii.2-3.

7 *Phys*. A4, 187b1-7.

8 *P.A*. B1, 646a13-24; *Mete*. Δ12, 389b23-8, 390b3-14.

9 *Met*. Z3, 1029a7-12. For the rest of this section I shall be commenting on the argument of this important chapter. For helpful discussion of the problems raised by the chapter, see M. Schofield, '*Metaph*. Z3: some suggestions', *Phronesis* 17 (1972), 97-101; H.M. Robinson, 'Prime Matter in Aristotle', *Phronesis* 19 (1974), 166-88; W. Charlton, *Aristotle's Physics I,II* (Oxford, 1970), pp.129-45.

10 *Met*. Z3, 1029a12-19; cf. *Phys*. A7, 191a7-12.

11 *Met*. Z3, 1029a26-30.

12 I believe that this is an important methodological principle for the history of philosophy; but a full defence cannot be attempted here. It requires that we should draw a sharp distinction between accusations of surface and of latent contradiction. There is clearly a connection with the notion of the Principle of Charity in contemporary philosophy of language; cf. D. Davidson, 'Thought and Talk', reprinted in *Inquiries into Truth and Interpretation* (Oxford, 1984), esp. pp.168-9.

13 *Met*. Z11, 1036b24-32; cf. Z8, 1033b19-29; Z17, 1041b4-9.

14 *Met*. H6, 1045a25-33.

15 *Met*. B3, 998b6-8; cf. Z6, 1031a28-b7.

16 *Met*. Z8, 1034a7-8; Λ8, 1074a33-5.

17 This is the thought which inspires his examination of essence in *Met*. Z4-6. In those chapters the topics of universals and Plato's Forms arise naturally and frequently (e.g. Z4, 1030a7-17; Z6, 1031b11-18).

18 The importance of this issue in interpretation has been stressed by M.J. Woods, 'Problems in *Metaphysics* Z, Chapter 13', in J.M.E. Moravcsik (ed.), *Aristotle: A Collection of Critical Essays* (New York, 1967), pp.215-38. This article contains a number of valuable insights which have influenced my own discussion.

19 *Met*. Z13, 1038b9-15; Z14, 1039a33-b2.

20 *Met*. Z13, 1038b23-34, 1039a7-10; Z14, 1039b9-17.

21 Berkeley, *Principles of Human Knowledge*, Introduction 11-13.

22 *Met*. Z14, 1039b2-6.

23 The opposition between individual things and objects of definition is argued in *Met*. Z15; cf. *Top*. Z6, 143b23-32.

24 P. Geach and M. Black (eds.), *The Philosophical Writings of Gottlob Frege* (Blackwell, 1960), pp. 32, 43, 54-5.

25 This suggestion is rejected at *Met*. Z16, 1040b16-27. But elsewhere Aristotle makes it clear that it is a serious theme in the universalist's repertoire; cf. *Met*. Z6, 1031b9-10; B3, 998b19-27.

26 Woods (see note 18 above) distinguishes *the universal* and *what is said universally* (p.229). I contest the legitimacy of this distinction; cf. *De Int*. 7, 17a38-b1.

27 *Met*. Z17, 1041b4-9, b26-8.

[28] This needs slight qualification. In some versions of the text there is a mention of 'form' at 1041b8. But most modern editors regard this as an insertion, not belonging to the original text; for a recent comment, see Burnyeat (note 3 above) p.154.

[29] This is argued for the case of Plato, from whom Aristotle took over the analogy with letters and syllable, by G. Ryle, 'Letters and Syllables in Plato', *Philosophical Review* 69 (1960), 431-51. For the phonetic bias in Aristotle, see *Met.* M10, 1086b23, 1087a7. When Aristotle discusses fallacies of language in *S.E.*, he is primarily thinking of spoken language; this is clear above all from his inclusion of the fallacy of accent (cf. *S.E.* 20, 177b2-8).

[30] *Met.* Z17, 1041b11-17, b30-3.

[31] For a trenchant discussion of this issue, see R.D. Sykes, 'Form in Aristotle: Universal or Particular?', *Philosophy* 50 (1975), 311-31. It will be clear that I reject his conclusion that Aristotle has no clear answer to the question.

[32] Cf. *Met.* M10, 1087a10-25; Θ8, 1050a15-16.

[33] For Aristotle's recognition of the usefulness, as well as the danger, of such abstractionist fictions, cf. *An. Post.* A24, 85a31-b3, b15-22, *Met.* M3, 1078a17-30.

[34] Cf. *Met.* Z4, 1030a10-13. The talk of what is 'primary' here provides a connection to the discussion of primary substance in the *Categories* (see Chapter 3, p.45 above), since the latter is introduced by a species-term, although not itself a species.

[35] The Greek word is '*eidos*'. A discussion which indicates very clearly the error in proposing an ambiguity is *Met.* Z10, where Aristotle debates whether material parts of a thing should be mentioned in its definition. What these are contrasted with is the *kind* of thing being defined, and the nature of the kind is provided by the *form*.

CHAPTER 5

Philosophy of Nature

Most substances are involved in change, as causes or as causally affected. The role of matter and form in the analysis of substance has been scrutinised in Chapter 4; but the conception of substance has been mainly of something static. We have tried to capture a substance at an instant of its temporal career, and to determine what is contributed to its nature by its material constituents and what, in turn, by the structural principles that organise this matter. We have sought to understand what it is for such a substance *to exist*.

This is a suitable aim for metaphysics. It seeks to understand things in respect of their existence.[1] But Aristotle recognises another, more restricted study of things, which he calls 'physics'—the study of natural substances and their properties. The domain of physics is more restricted than metaphysics. If there should happen to be something which is free from involvement in change, this is a proper subject for metaphysics but not for physics; there is no item in the subject matter of physics which is unavailable to metaphysics.[2] Even if the domains of the two studies should turn out to be coextensive, metaphysics would still have the priority. It studies things as things, while physics studies them in respect of their involvement in change.[3]

But change is no accidental feature of natural substances. It is of great importance to keep this in view as we study them. If the metaphysical investigations said anything that conflicted with that insight, it would seriously undermine their worth. One of Aristotle's main complaints against Plato is that his attempt to study reality almost completely ignores the fact of change.

By contrast, Aristotle's metaphysical theory gives prominence to the very factors that will play a crucial role in the analysis of change. The most notable among them are matter and form and the associated notions of potentiality and actuality. The ground is prepared for the dynamic analysis of natural substances which animates Aristotle's vast range of work in the philosophy of nature—the *Physics*, and the treatises on astronomy, chemistry, biology and psychology.[4]

Aristotle devotes several major discussions to the analysis of causes; it will help us to understand why, if we bear in mind the central role of change in his philosophy of nature. 'Cause' is a conventional translation of a key term in Aristotle. This word may strike us as strange, accustomed as we are to Hume's analysis of causality. An easier way to approach Aristotle's discussions would be to translate the work as 'ground' or 'explanatory factor'.[5] But to fail to see his account as a direct rival to alternative theories of causality, including Hume's, would be a mistake. Aristotle is at pains to confront the contemporary versions of such theories and to show that they are inferior to his own. His philosophy of nature has attracted considerable contumely. It exercised great influence over many centuries; and the faithful adherence which it evoked, led eventually to equally severe rejection. Aristotle is not to be blamed for the servility of his erstwhile followers. His ideas outlive the disputes which have made his acolytes' systems unfashionable.[6]

A centrepiece of this philosophy is the doctrine of the four causes. The four kinds of causal factor are: material, formal, efficient and final. These names refer to the stuff of which a thing is made, the structure by which it is organised, the source of change, and the purpose or end.[7] Information about a thing under any of these headings will contribute to its explanation; and when all four kinds of causal factor are detailed, we shall have a complete explanation.

This is a wider notion of causal explanation than the one familiar to us. Aristotle's third heading—the efficient cause or the source of change—corresponds fairly obviously to our idea of cause, but the other headings seem alien. The builder is the cause of the house, of course, but it seems senseless to say that the bricks and mortar are causes also. Nonetheless Aristotle argues that his wider conception is the correct one; in particular he maintains that there are neither more nor fewer than these four types of cause, and that without a grasp of this it is impossible to provide an adequate explanation of natural objects and events.[8]

Change: Matter and Form

Modern analytical philosophy concerns itself rather little with change. Most Greek philosophers took it as a central and deeply troublesome phenomenon. While some were prepared to dismiss all change as an illusion, others did not go this far; but they sought to reduce radical versions of change to more amenable forms. All his philosophical predecessors, in Aristotle's view, failed to face up to the importance of change in natural substances. The clue to a proper conception lies with the notions of matter and form.

With a radical change one thing turns into another, so that it is appropriate to speak of the destruction of the first and the creation of the second. With a non-radical change the one thing endures through the change, in the course of which it acquires a new quality, size or location. My distinction between radical and non-radical change parallels Aristotle's distinction between change of substance and change in other categories.[9]

The general problem of change may be broached by considering the non-radical variety—for example, the change of a person's complexion from pale to sunburnt. What exactly is the change here? The person persists through the change and undergoes no alteration of personal identity; equally the complexions are unaffected, since neither sunburn nor pallor changes in this process. One is tempted to say that what changes is none of the items so far considered but rather the presence or absence of these complexions in the person. But the three factors—the person, sunburn, pallor—do seem to represent the only possible candidates for where the change takes place; and even if we admit the presence and absence of the attribute as further candidates, it is no more plausible to claim that these undergo change. So we want to say that there is a change but not that any particular element in the situation changes; and this is paradoxical.[10]

Aristotle compares and contrasts two ways of describing our specimen change. On the one hand, we can say that the pale person becomes a sunburnt person; on the other, we can speak of his pallor turning to sunburn.[11] The first of these conveys too little sense of change and the second too much. Yet they appear to be alternative ways of expressing the same fact. We shall not understand such change unless we can explain how the two statements are equivalent and how neither misrepresents the nature of change.

According to one conception of change there may seem to be no problem. All that is needed for us to be satisfied that a thing has changed is a change in the truth-value of a statement describing it. This account of change allows some cases to count as 'changes' where we would not readily accept that a thing has changed at all. If, for example, some thing becomes or ceases to be an object of admiration to creatures of which it is completely unaware, this will mean an alteration in the truth of statements about the thing; and yet the thing itself may not have changed at all.

For this reason some philosophers have rejected the proposed criterion of change, giving it and the changes which it lets in the label 'Cambridge' (because of the academic environment from which it originated).[12] Aristotle rejects it too. He calls such changes accidental, meaning not that they happen by accident but that it is an accident that they are changes. A change such as becoming an object of admiration, only happens to be a change; and this *does* happen because a real change is involved elsewhere in the situation.[13]

The Cambridge way of escaping the difficulty over non-radical change is not acceptable to Aristotle. Yet this was precisely the prospect which seduced those of his predecessors who wished to recast radical as non-radical change. Radical change raises even more starkly the question of which element in the situation actually changes. Certainly some imaginable radical changes could only be construed on the Cambridge model. Suppose that the existence of this book was immediately succeeded, without perceptible spatio-temporal gap, by a tiger. Would this be a case of a book changing into a tiger? Presumably not. In order to be satisfied that this was genuinely a change and not just a remarkable succession of one state of affairs by another, we should need to discover some factor which leads from the one to the other.[14] This, we may note provisionally, sounds like a demand for a cause.

We shall not secure an adequate insight into radical change by restricting ourselves to change in the truth-value of statements as a criterion. It is necessary to find elements of continuity between the states of affairs at either term of the change. But Aristotle insists that it is *radical* change which we are trying to understand. Perhaps a book turning into a tiger is not an example of this; but wood turning into smoke, or grass turning into flesh are. Yet in these cases, no less than in the impossible one, one substance is destroyed and another created, so that the latter is substituted for the former.

Aristotle's predecessors sought to meet this difficulty by analysing radical on the model of non-radical change. They postulated some underlying substance which is refashioned in the change. The Atomists, for example, argued that a rearrangement of the same basic enduring atoms could produce distinct substances; so in the change from wood to smoke the atoms remain but their phenomenal form alters. But such an analysis cannot stand as an explanation of radical change. It explains it away. Aristotle's own account of change differs notably from the reductionism of the Atomists, Plato and other precursors.

For a correct analysis of radical change three factors are needed—matter, form and privation.[15] We encountered the first two in the investigation of substance in the previous chapter. Privation is a less evident part of Aristotle's conceptual armoury. It is exemplified by such attributes as blindness or lameness.[16] These represent the absence of some characteristic; but since their application is restricted to subjects whose nature it is to have the characteristic, they are not merely negative. Kant recognised the importance of this concept by assigning it to his qualitative category of limitation.[17] Aristotle's use of the concept is much more significant.

The account of radical change can now be stated very simply. A substance is a combination of matter and form. For it to be destroyed is for the matter to shed the form and to assume the privation; and for it to be created is for the matter to take on the form, having lost the privation. In such change the matter persists and is characterised successively by form and privation. Matter, form and privation in this account correspond to the subject and the two contrary attributes—the person, pallor, sunburn—in the analysis of non-radical change.[18]

So far we have an account that assimilates radical to non-radical change, thereby lessening the extra mystery which the former is felt to have in relation to the latter. But the discussion must be taken further to resolve two issues. There remains the problem, for both kinds of change, of explaining what real change consists in; and there is a need to provide an effective basis for the conviction that some changes are radical—that is, that they mark a transition from one substance to a different, wholly new one.

The problem with the change from a pale person to a sunburnt person was that no single one of the three elements in the situation was judged suitable as the location of the change—neither the person, since he persists, nor the opposed attributes, since they do not change into each other. But once we see that the solution must be derived from these three elements, it is readily to hand. The following are true: the person who is pale becomes a person who is sunburnt, and the pallor in the person becomes sunburn in that person. The following, however, are false: the person becomes a different thing, and pallor becomes sunburn. The true statements are distinguished from the false by the descriptions under which the items which change are presented. Provided that the role played by each of three elements is correctly reflected in the description of the change, we can avoid becoming embroiled in the difficulties posed by alternative descriptions which suggest that either too much or too little change occurs in these cases.[19]

These lessons should be applied to the analysis of radical change, emphasising the parallel between it and non-radical change. Here too, what makes the difference between an acceptable and an unacceptable account is the descriptions under which the various items are presented. If we describe the change in such a way that it seems simply to consist of a form turning into a privation or vice versa, this is as unintelligible as the 'change' of a book into a tiger; and if we refer to the matter in the description of the change, it will not be possible to indicate that any *change* is occurring, since this is a factor which remains constant throughout the change.[20] But the task of keeping the three factors in correct perspective is harder in the case of radical change; and this is why a clear realisation that three factors are involved is essential.

We need to bear in mind a semantic consequence of the ontological analysis, detailed in Chapter 4, of the relation between matter and form. The terms by which we designate substances are typically ambiguous between matter and form, although it is Aristotle's leading thesis that in their primary use, in the absence of indications to the contrary, they designate form rather than matter.[21] The terms have these meanings because the matter actually exists only when it possesses form. When we speak of wood becoming smoke, we mention all three elements needed for a radical change, since we are using terms which are ambiguous in the way in which they designate these elements. 'Wood' designates both the material substrate which persists through the change *and* the form which it assumes at one term of the change. The success of Aristotle's analysis depends on recognising this semantic complexity. It is a mistake to suppose that in the canonical description of a radical change, the subject word designates the matter to the exclusion of the form or the reverse. There is a reference to both matter and form in the use of 'wood' to introduce a subject of change. Thus we avoid inadequate conceptions of change which result from identifying the subject exclusively with either of these elements in the meaning of the word which designates it.

If the account of radical change parallels that of the non-radical variety, how is it that they also differ significantly? The views just canvassed about matter and form, and the meanings of terms for substances, resolve this difficulty too. We noted that the primary meaning of such a term is the form, not the matter. This reading of the language of radical change immediately introduces a disanalogy with non-radical change.[22] In the latter case the correct way to describe the change is by using as the subject the name of the thing that persists through the change, as in 'the person becomes sunburnt'. But to construe a sentence like 'the wood becomes smoke' in this way is, Aristotle maintains, precisely the mistake of the Atomists. It is to interpret all such change in terms of the rearrangement of enduring and continuously identifiable material substrates, which are named by the subjects in sentences describing what such substrates become. This interpretation presents radical change entirely after the pattern of non-radical change, the only difference coming from the obviousness with which the enduring subject can be discerned.

Aristotle, on the other hand, construes the subject word in a description of radical change as primarily designating the form but not in such a way as to exclude the matter; the reference is to the form of that matter. When we speak of wood becoming smoke, 'wood' means the form and the change is the replacement of this by another form. What then, to repeat our earlier problem about radical change, makes this replacement a *change*? The answer is that 'wood' also designates the matter which is actualised in the form wood. This matter persists through the change to smoke, so that after the change the wood, in this material sense, is smoke; only, this is merely potentially wood, something that is capable through a series of appropriate radical changes of assuming again the form of wood.[23] This account cannot be extended to cover any radical replacement which we would not allow as a change; and this confirms the rightness of Aristotle's analysis.

Causation

Aristotle's theory of change assigns great importance to the notions of matter and form. Not only does the distinction between matter and form in general serve as the foundation of a correct analysis of change; the particular properties of the matter and form involved in each change are essential for understanding how it can come about. The factors which go to make a thing what it is—matter and form—are also crucial to an accurate account of what it can become.[24] For this reason Aristotle includes matter and form as two of the basic elements in the explanation of a thing, as two of its 'causes'. An Aristotelian substance must be construed dynamically, as was argued earlier; we cannot know what it is and yet ignore the processes of change in which it is involved. Plato thought that change was a bar to the intelligibility of substances; and in taking this view he reflected the bias among earlier philosophers against taking seriously the reality of change. Aristotle insists that the analysis of natural substances should do full justice to their mutability.

The other two kinds of cause are the efficient and the final, the source of change and the end purpose. More obviously than matter and form these causes introduce factors which are responsible for events; but while what Aristotle says is clear, it is not at all easy to accept. His leading thesis is that the main direction of causation is backwards, from future to present or past;[25] and this view runs counter to ideas about events and causes which many later philosophers have taken to be so fundamental as to be analytic or *a priori*.[26] Once again we shall see that these ideas are prefigured in the philosophical background to Aristotle's work too.

Two general questions may be asked about any event: Where did it start from? Where is it heading? The modern view of the explanation of events is that the notion of cause is defined by the significance of the first question and the insignificance of the second. Aristotle approaches the issue in the reverse order. A full sense of the complexity of the notion of cause comes from realising that the questions are distinct, and that answers to both of them are essential for a proper understanding of the event. In addition the role of matter and form must be considered.

In essence Aristotle's theory of four causes has two aspects. In the first place, it acknowledges complexity where earlier accounts oversimplified. His complaint against his predecessors is that they concentrated on one or other of the types of cause, in the mistaken belief that this was sufficient to exhaust the question.[27] This shortsightedness led them to engage in unproductive disputes about the propriety of recognising any kind of cause other than their favoured candidate. Plato, for example, rejected material causes because he believed that all causal explanation should proceed exclusively in terms of form. Aristotle comments that even if Plato is correct about the importance in causality of form, he is wrong to deny significance to all other causal factors. Analysis shows that an adequate explanation of some object or event must consist of not one but four parts, even if on occasion the same factor may serve as cause under more than one of the four headings.

Aristotle's theory is not just conceptual analysis of causality. For, secondly, a substantive thesis is advanced as to which of the four causes has priority. This, he argues, is the final cause; the causal thesis is teleology. The most important of the four causes is the purpose or end result. While a full account of a thing's cause requires explanations under all four headings, the final cause will provide the deepest insight into why it occurs.[28]

Well aware that this thesis is controversial, Aristotle has three lines of argument in defence of it. We may label these: scientific, conceptual, metaphysical. The scientific defence points to a host of actual phenomena in the world which are more satisfactorily and comprehensively explained through teleology than through other causal theories. The claim here is that whatever problems in the concept of cause may still have to be ironed out, teleology works. The conceptual defence addresses these problems by arguing that the things which we are aiming to explain causally, have certain logical features which make final causes specially suitable for such explanation. Even if we lacked the factual data which support the scientific defence, this claim would command interest. The metaphysical defence confronts certain philosophical problems surrounding the whole notion of causality. The first two defences may have done much to justify the application of final causation to the explanation of particular cases; but there are quite general difficulties, intensified by alternative philosophical theories, in the idea that the direction of causation can be from later to earlier time. Unless these difficulties are resolved, the considerations in the first two defences should not satisfy us that purposes or ends can be causes of the phenomena which precede them.

The very deep problems raised by this last area of argument will be held over to Chapter 6. Now I shall examine the scientific and the conceptual arguments; and the considerations which emerge will clarify and justify the dynamic view of natural substances already advanced.

Teleology

Most of Aristotle's work in natural science is in the broad field of biology; and this is where he finds the major support for the thesis that end-product determines antecedent process. His main argument depends on the fact that living creatures develop true to kind.[29] It is natural to infer that the stage-by-stage process of the creature's development is controlled by the nature of the final state in which the process will terminate. Such variation as there is, is mostly observed in the earlier rather than the later stages of the development. So it looks as if what is causally, even if not temporally, prior is the state that comes at the end, not at the beginning; degrees of similarity among the various stages of the process are explained by their proximity to the causally basic factor.

Aristotle has much to say about the artistry and purposiveness of nature. Two warnings against misinterpretation are necessary: he regards nature piecemeal, not as a unitary whole; and he means purposiveness of an unconscious, 'as if' kind, and is not attributing conscious purpose to all substances—non-human animals and plants, as well as more elemental forms—which exhibit purposive change.[30] His account is not to be attacked for claims which it does not in fact make. Even so, it seems remarkably unattractive.

In the more polemical passages in defence of teleology the main target is Empedocles. His theory was a somewhat undeveloped version of the mechanism which we have already encountered in the Atomists. Empedocles maintained that all gross substances of ordinary observation are compounds of elemental substances (the same four as Aristotle's elements plus two morally motivating factors). Aristotle took Empedocles as a representative of a tendency to base biology on a theory of the survival of the fittest.[31] Those who adopted this theory did not dispute the evidence of purposiveness which so impressed Aristotle, but they explained it by non-purposive causal mechanisms. Earlier states of affairs give rise to later ones. It is mere chance if some of these processes produce effects which suggest purpose and contrivance, and equally a matter of chance if such effects are numerically predominant because of the unfitness of other products to survive.

The Empedoclean theory sought to accommodate the observed facts of purpose in nature without recourse to teleology. It is still likely to be preferred to Aristotle's theory; the Darwinism that colours our intellectual climate reproduces the essentials of Empedocles' idea, supplementing it simply with a far fuller and more convincing account of the causal processes which produce the appearance of contrivance.[32] This theory provides the intellectual context in which Aristotle advances his scientific argument for teleology. What he finds particularly unsatisfactory in the mechanist position is the use it makes of—and the importance it attaches to—the notion of chance.

Detailed observation of living natural substances does not support the view that the operation of chance is widespread. Aristotle notes how we find the same parts and processes performing more than one vital function in the substance which they constitute. Life-preserving functions, such as breathing and eating, are carried out by the same organs as are needed to fulfil other functions, such as perception or locomotion, which are also essential to a particular kind of life. Cross-specific comparisons can assist these observations; an elephant's trunk, for example, functions as a nose does in other animals, but also serves locomotive purposes, thereby indicating how different ends can be achieved by a single organ.[33] The converse proposition can also be supported. Apparently useless parts and processes are shown to contribute to the animal's total life-functions, often by comparison with other species where the role of the problematic factor is clearer.[34] The economy of effort which goes into securing advantageous results is emphasised throughout these investigations.

These two features of biological reality—the use of limited materials to perform a number of functions, and the avoidance of redundant materials—are summed up by Aristotle's frequent remark that 'nature does nothing in vain or to excess'.[35] He maintains that the extraordinarily neat match between the available materials and their roles in expediting life-functions completely belies the Empedoclean claim that such connections are due to chance. If we assemble a lot of different mechanical parts, they might indeed prove useful in the construction of some complex machine. But unless the assemblage were determined by a forward plan of the finished machine, inevitably some parts would be missing and others left over. Aristotle is not afraid of the analogy between nature and art, provided we remember that in nature we need no artist. Given the relation between process and product, in neither case is it credible that the former issues in the latter by chance.

These results of observation in biology, Aristotle believes, extend to the non-living substances studied in other parts of natural science. Elemental substances and sub-living chemical compounds behave in a goal-directed way; their natural movements are determined by the regions of the universe where it is natural for them to reside.[36] For example, it is natural for earth to be concentrated at the centre of the universe, and fire at its periphery; so the evident downward movement of earth and upward movement of fire are finally—purposively—caused by the locations in which it is their nature to end up. The details of this line of thought are most thoroughly exploited in the astronomical work *De Caelo*; they are used in support of a more ambitious argument in the fundamental philosophy of nature, to be examined in Chapter 10.

The application of teleology to physics is one of the most notorious features of Aristotle's natural science. If Darwinism has discredited his biology, his physics has been demolished by the dynamics of Galileo and Newton. This aspect of Aristotle's teleology is best defended by the conceptual argument, which we shall consider shortly; but there is an important reason why he should not need to mount any special scientific argument for the purposiveness of physical and chemical entities. Such substances typically attain actual existence only if they are organised into more complex substances; and the more complex substances are those studied by biology. In other words, substances such as earth and iron are actualised through organisation (in combination with other substances) into the tissues and organs of living creatures.[37] If the latter are susceptible to teleological analysis, this will simultaneously serve as a causal explanation of more elemental substances too. Aristotle's programme of explanation in natural science is 'top-down'. This is why he does not articulate the philosophy of nature into the modern divisions of physics, chemistry, biology (botany and zoology) and psychology.

I turn now to the second main defence of teleology; this is the conceptual argument. Let us amplify what was said earlier about the distinctness of the four causes. Aristotle meant that they represent different kinds of explanatory account. He insists that confusion over the aims of explanation is the result of failing to grasp these differences. It does not follow that in every case there will be a different cause under each of the four headings.

In fact Aristotle maintains that the same item will often be efficient, formal and final cause.[38] Thus the processes which constitute the life of an animal are caused by the natural kind to which it belongs, which also supplies the end result of these processes and, through the reproductive activity of the parent member of the same species, their origin. Formal, final and efficient causes are essentially the same here, the only difference being the numerical one that it is not the same member of the species which is both efficient and formal/final cause.

The frequent coincidence of form with purpose proves the logical priority of final over efficient causes. It is noteworthy that when we name or describe processes, we do so in terms of their result rather than their origin. Building a house and running a mile are processes which are most appropriately described by specifying the state in which they terminate, not the one from which they start.[39] This point strikes us forcefully when we reflect on processes which fail to reach their final state. If someone collapses while running a mile, he does not run a mile. Yet running a mile is the process which was thwarted by the collapse; and even in a case like this we do not redescribe it in terms of what unproblematically did occur, namely the beginning of the run.[40]

Aristotle argues that non-realisation of purpose also occurs with some natural processes. In such cases the end-result is used to describe the process even though the result is not actually achieved. He infers that these habits of speech and thought indicate the essential nature of such processes; they are purposive, where this is to be construed as entailing neither that the purpose is consciously entertained nor that it is actually realised. What is growing into an oak tree may yet fail actually to become an oak tree. From the teleological standpoint Aristotle describes this as a case in which the thing's development into an oak tree is frustrated. The conceptual argument for teleology notes the consequence: since it is natural to speak of a process of growing into an oak tree, even when none actually results, the true nature of the process stands revealed as directed towards an end result.[41]

Natural processes, then, share with human activities the logical feature that they are characteristically described by the end to which they tend rather than the origin from which they start. We shall understand and explain them most thoroughly by referring to the end-result; and the conceptual relation between causality and explanation in Aristotle means that to say this is to assign primacy to the final cause.

Potentiality and Actuality

Another important element in Aristotle's whole analysis of change which supports this conclusion is his distinction between actuality and potentiality, between what a thing actually is and what it is capable of being. The language by which we describe things is pervasively ambiguous between the senses of actuality and potentiality.[42] To speak of something as running fast or evenly balanced is not necessarily to describe the current actual condition of the thing; it may mean only that the thing is capable of exhibiting these characteristics. This distinction is fundamental to Aristotle's conception of change and, indeed, to his defence of its possibility.

Change is defined as 'the actualisation of the potential qua potential'.[43] This somewhat rebarbative phrase means that it is a precondition for any change that its subject must first be capable of bearing the characteristic which the change will impart to it. The process of heating can be undergone only by subjects capable of becoming hot; the change occurs in respect of this feature of their nature, and it results in the subject's actually being hot. Simple as this insight is, however, it is open to a misconstruction which some of Aristotle's contemporaries thought could be exploited to undermine the very possibility of change. It is not coherent, they argued, to suppose it possible for something not hot to be hot; for being both hot and not hot is not a possible condition of anything.[44]

The first thing to say about this argument is that it commits an elementary blunder in the way it construes the scope of the modal terms involved. To say that it is possible for something which is not hot to be hot, can be construed so as to give wide scope to the word 'possible'; in that case the claim will be false. The alternative, more natural reading assigns the word narrow scope; it says about what is actually not hot that it has the possibility to be hot. Aristotle was alert to such ambiguity of scope;[45] but his modal theory goes further than merely observing that statements of possibility can be interpreted in this way. His theory of potentiality gives primacy to a narrow scope interpretation; potentialities are real properties of objects, and according to the definition of change they set the limits within which objects can change.[46]

Armed with this theory Aristotle is able to solve several puzzles which had provoked extravagant responses from his predecessors. Plato in the *Meno* had noted the difficulty of explaining how it is possible for a person to *learn* anything, given certain natural ways of characterising knowledge and ignorance. It seems that the person must either know or be ignorant of any item which is a candidate for being learnable; but if he knows it, he cannot learn it, and if he is ignorant of it, the object of his search is unclear, so that in either case the possibility of learning is excluded. Plato's response was to maintain that in one sense or another the learner really knows all along what he learns. Aristotle finds this unsatisfactory as a solution, and indicative of an inadequate grasp of the problem. It is the latter point that concerns us now. Plato's discussion is wanting because it does not reflect our conviction that whatever else learning is, it is a *change*.

The only way to meet this requirement is by the notion of potentiality.[47] Learning depends on the possession by the ignorant of a potentiality for knowledge. We shall not make the mistake of construing the talk of potentiality here as being of wide scope. That would lead us back to the idea, which forms part of the basis of the problem in the *Meno*, of attributing to the learner the contradiction of both knowing and being ignorant. Rather, Aristotle's theory maintains that among the properties which a subject possesses are potentialities which, were they to be actualised, would be incompatible with certain other of its properties. Before he starts to learn, a person is actually ignorant, but this does not rule out his possessing a potentiality for knowledge. Should this potentiality be actualised, the person's condition *then* will, of course, be incompatible with one of actual ignorance; but this poses no difficulty.

This example shows how in the analysis of change—and in the defence of that analysis against destructive paradox—a very important role is played by the notion of a potential property.

The conceptual argument for teleological explanation gains further support. A potential property is one which can be defined only by reference to the result to which it tends. The defence of the possibility of learning relies on the notion of knowledge, which is the final cause of the process.

When we say this, we are not merely underwriting the truism that processes have origins and terminations. If that were so, the argument would provide no special support for teleology, since the logical role of the originating state—ignorance, in the example of learning—would be as important as that of the terminal state. The point, rather, is that the process depends essentially on *potentialities*; and these are not symmetrical with respect to earlier and later times. The only potentiality that arises here is one for the later state. This is the special way in which the future determines the nature of a process which precedes it.

For a sharper idea of Aristotle's thinking on this issue, let us consider another example of change. This is the case of mixture.[48] Aristotle emphasises that mixture is not to be confused with juxtaposition, in which particles of some amount of stuff are aggregated with those of some other amount, for example grains of sand with crumbs of bread. But if mixture is a more thorough change than that, there arise problems analogous to those we considered in the case of learning. Suppose two components are to be combined in a mixture, there are three possibilities: either both are preserved, or both are destroyed, or one is preserved and one is destroyed. But none of these corresponds to a correct conception of mixture. Mixture is not juxtaposition, which rules out the first possibility. Nor is it radical change, since the ingredients are extractable from the mixture, so that the third possibility is excluded. The second possibility sums the disadvantages of the other two.[49]

The only way out of the impasse is to recognise that the presence or absence of the ingredients in the mixture is not an all-or-nothing matter. Introduce the distinction between potentiality and actuality, and this will allow us to distinguish different senses in which the ingredients remain the same and become different before, during and after mixture. Their potentialities are as much part of the ingredients' natures as are the actual states which they exhibit from time to time; so the fact that they retain the potentialities through changes of actual state will satisfy the requirement that they remain the same as well as becoming different.[50] Of course, this would be too glib if Aristotle did not provide further conditions which a genuine potentiality must satisfy; and he does this later in the analysis.[51] For our present argument the important point is to see the detailed use which Aristotle makes of the notion of potentiality to resolve a specific problem about those changes which are mixtures; without this notion mixtures could still be changes but not precisely the kind of change which in fact they are.

As with learning, in the analysis of mixture potentiality is potentiality for a particular future state. There are certain properties which a thing must have if it is to be a component in a mixture, and the predicates designating these properties make essential reference to states which lie in the subject's future. So what a thing later is to become determines the correct description, for someone who studies its changes, of what it currently is. Thus we see how the later stage is conceptually prior to the earlier.

Notes

1 *Met.* Γ1; E1, 1025b3-13.
2 *Met.* E1, 1025b18-21; Λ1, 1069a30-b2: *P.A.* A1. 641a33-b10.
3 *Met.* K3, 1061b6-7.
4 *Mete.* A1, 338a20-25, 339a7-9.
5 Cf. W. Charlton, *Aristotle's Physics I, II* (Oxford, 1970), pp.98-9; R.R.K. Sorabji, *Necessity, Cause and Blame* (London, 1980), pp.40-2. Both commentators, particularly Sorabji, also note the connections between Aristotle's ideas and later theories.
6 Aristotle was certainly confident that his answers to most questions would be hard to improve on (cf. *S.E.* 34, 183b23-8). But we should also remember the lesson of Chapter 1, that philosophy thrives on disagreement; later thinkers who took him as an authority missed this aspect of his philosophy.
7 *Phys.* B3, 194b23-5a3; *Met.* A3, 983a26-32.
8 *Phys.* B7, 198a21-4.
9 *Phys.* E1, 225b5-9; *G.C.* A2, 317a17-27; A4, 319b6-18.
10 The problem is most thoroughly examined in *Phys.* A7-9. An excellent recent discussion is provided by S. Waterlow, *Nature, Change, and Agency in Aristotle's Physics* (Oxford, 1982), esp. pp.5-28.
11 *Phys.* A7, 190a21-31.
12 See P.T. Geach, 'God's Relation to the World', repr. in *Logic Matters* (Blackwell, 1972), pp.321-3.

13 *Phys*. E1, 224b18-20, 26-8.
14 *Phys*. A7, 190b1-10; cf. *Met*. Z7, 1032b26-32.
15 *Phys*. A7, 190b23-30; *Met*. Λ2, 1069b32-4.
16 *Cat*. 10, 12a26-b25.
17 *Critique of Pure Reason* B111; cf. A72-3/B97-8.
18 *Met*. Λ4, 1070b16-21.
19 *Phys*. A7, 190a13-21.
20 *Phys*. A7, 190b35-1a3; A8, 191b10-18.
21 *G.C*. A5, 321b19-22; cf. *Phys*. A8, 191b27-34.
22 In a number of passages (*Met*. Z7, 1033a5-22; Θ7; *Phys*. H3, 245b3-6a9) Aristotle draws a subtle linguistic distinction between the appropriateness of nouns and of adjectives to describe certain changes, e.g. a distinction between the uses of 'wood' and 'wooden' where wood is involved in a change. He argues that the adjectival form is the more accurate way to characterise both a qualitative attribute in relation to its subject *and* matter in relation to form.
23 For the thesis that all substances, directly or indirectly, can change into each other, see *G.C*. B5, 332b27-32; B10, 337a1-7; B11, 338b6-19.
24 *De An*. A1, 403a24-b12; *Met*. E1, 1025b28-6a6.
25 *P.A*. B1, 646a25-b10; A1, 640a3-6.
26 Cf. M.A.E. Dummett, 'Can an Effect Precede its Cause?', repr. in *Truth and Other Enigmas* (London, 1978), p.319: 'The thought that an effect might precede its cause appears at first nonsensical.'
27 *Met*. A7, 988a33-5, b6-16.
28 *P.A*. A1, 639b12-21.
29 *Phys*. B8, 198b32-9a8, 199b14-26.
30 *Phys*. B8, 199b26-33; cf. *P.A*. A1, 639b19-21, for the idea that the lack of an actual artist makes nature more artful than art.
31 *P.A*. A1, 640a19-27; *Phys*. B8, 198b23-32; *G.C*. B6, 333a16-b18.
32 Cf. W.K.C. Guthrie, *A History of Greek Philosophy* vol. 2 (Cambridge, 1965), pp.203-5.
33 *P.A*. B16, 658b27-9a29.
34 A good example of this is provided by the discussion of the neck in serpents (*P.A*. Δ11, 691b28-2a8); comparison with other animals establishes not only (what is far from obvious) that serpents do have a neck, but also what role it plays in their lives.
35 *G.A*. B6, 744a37-8; cf. *Cael*. B12, 291b13-14.
36 *Cael*. A2, 268b14-16; *Phys*. Δ4, 211a4-6.
37 *Met*. Z16, 1040b5-16; cf. *G.C*. A5, 321b28-34.
38 *Phys*. B7, 198a24-6.
39 *P.A*. B1, 646b3-4; cf. *Phys*. Γ1, 201b5-15.
40 For discussion of this kind of example, see G.E.L. Owen, 'Particular and General', *Proceedings of the Aristotelian Society* 79 (1978-79), p.18.
41 Aristotle discusses this phenomenon under the heading of 'deformity' (cf. *G.A*. A18, 724b32-5; B3, 737a18-30); and his approach is teleological even though in these cases purpose is frustrated.
42 *Met*. Δ7, 1017a35-b9; N2, 1089a28-31.
43 *Phys*. Γ1, 201a9-19; Θ5, 257b6-10.

44 *Met*. Θ3, 1046b29-32, 1047a10-17. For some discussion of this argument, see S. Waterlow, *Passage and Possibility* (Oxford, 1982), pp.27-8, and R.R.K. Sorabji, *Necessity, Cause and Blame* (London, 1980), pp.135-7.

45 *S.E.* 4, 166a23-30; 20, 177a33-8.

46 For the specialised narrow scope notion (which some commentators misleadingly refer to by 'power' as opposed to 'potentiality'), see *Met*. Δ12, 1019b15-30.

47 Aristotle alludes to the problem of learning at *Met*. Θ3, 1046b36-7a3; for the general philosophical importance of the problem, see Chapter 1, pp.4-5 above.

48 *G.C.* A10.

49 *G.C.* A10, 327a34-b6.

50 *G.C.* A10, 327b27-31.

51 *G.C.* A10, 328a18-b14. These refinements concern the precise nature of the causal role played by each component in the mixture.

CHAPTER 6

Necessity and Chance

The main elements of Aristotle's theories of change and causation were examined in Chapter 5. This involved reference to both conceptual and empirical (i.e. scientific) issues. There is no sharp division between these two kinds of consideration; and this is consistent with what we learned about Aristotle's philosophical method in Chapter 1. It was also argued there that the central role played by conflicts in prevailing views is what distinguishes philosophy from science. Dialectical confrontation between alternative treatments of causality is the theme of Aristotle's third main defence of teleology, which I have labelled 'metaphysical'.

However plausible the first two defences discussed in the previous chapter may seem, it can still be objected that his account is deeply unsatisfying as an analysis of *causes*. Since causation is the cement of change,[1] a serious defect in the account of causation casts doubt on the basic thesis that natural substances are essentially involved in change. By Aristotle's lights as in subsequent theory, the concepts of cause and change are interdependent. So if he fails to explicate causation, his account of substance is bound to be one more entry in the list of Greek theories which interpret substances as independent of, and therefore immune to, change.

The Problem

Aristotle does not evade the issue. His response consists of a reasoned defence of the compatibility and truth of the following four propositions.

(1) Everything is explicable by one or more of the four kinds of cause;
(2) Everything occurs of necessity;
(3) Some things occur by chance;
(4) Determinism is false.

These four statements seem hard to reconcile with each other; and they read all the more oddly when viewed from the perspective of modern theory of causation, as it has developed from the work of Hume and Kant. Yet it was Aristotle who provided the original impetus for all later thinking about causation; and so it is of the first importance to work through his reasons for maintaining his heterodox fourfold set.

I shall briefly explain each proposition and then examine the reasons why Aristotle supports them. (1) expresses his claim to completeness in his analysis of causes. Parallel claims could be made out even if the particular kinds of cause recognised by Aristotle were contested; but we shall see that his defence of propositions (3) and (4) depends on the detailed theory behind his claim (1). The main thought in (1) is that a causal theory is adequate only if in principle it contains no gaps. This idea is supported by proposition (2). It is an ideal of causal theory to show that any item to be explained could not, given the factors adduced in the explanation, be other than it is. This thesis should not be interpreted so that it involves more than relative necessity, as we shall see; the item under explanation is necessary *given* the factors identified as causes. But Aristotle insists that a claim to have discovered a cause is defeated by its failure to necessitate the effect.[2]

If (1) and (2) hang together, so also do (3) and (4). In defence of (3) Aristotle points to the occurrence of exceptions to the regularities which causal analysis reveals. To say that these occur by chance is not to construe them as caused by chance. Their fortuitous character puts them outside the normal framework of causal analysis; and one confusion that Aristotle seeks to expose is precisely that of proposing chance as a cause. Any diagnosis of chance in the particular case may be defeated by further investigation of causes. But Aristotle has an argument to show that such investigation must peter out and leave a residue of items which cannot be fully handled by causal analysis.[3] In that case we should certainly be satisfied of the truth of proposition (4). It is sometimes argued that a fully-fledged causal theory, of the kind presupposed by proposition (1), does not entail determinism; we shall find that this is Aristotle's view too. However, a far easier route to the falsehood of determinism is provided by the defence of (3).

'Determinism' is a label that is unknown to Aristotle. Somewhat paradoxically, his conception of it is purer than that of many later philosophers, who have hedged it round with qualifications and complications. There is dialectical advantage in the plain and straightforward way in which determinism is presented as one seductive strand in a confused area of theory.[4] In discussing his version of (4), Aristotle's target is simply that everything is unconditionally necessary; and like most other contributors to the debate before or since, he sees the ensuing problem primarily, though not exclusively, as one involving human decision and action. He is convinced that a commonsense commitment to human choice and responsibility is correct; he opposes determinism and so supports proposition (4), interpreting this as requiring the adoption of an anti-determinist view of causation beyond the purely human sphere.[5]

The most surprising feature of Aristotle's theory is that it combines (1) and (2) with (3) and (4). We shall see that the work of effecting this reconciliation is done mainly by his teleology, and I shall argue that this fact constitutes the metaphysical defence of that approach to causal explanation. We need first to consider his amplification of the claim for completeness in the four kinds of cause—proposition (1). Any factor which is identified as a cause in one of the ways provided by the theory, can be picked out by a number of descriptions; so a statement of cause using one of the variant descriptions will also be true, provided the initial attribution of cause is correct. Let it be true that the (efficient) cause of a house is Callias, the builder. Then given that the builder is also a doctor, a man, and a living creature, there will be a true statement presenting each of these as the cause of the house.[6]

But this does not, of course, mean that all of these things are different kinds of cause, not even that they are all different efficient causes. Aristotle opposes the suggestion by spelling out their relation to what he originally gave as the cause—the builder. Some of the other items are more general kinds under which the builder falls, while others are things with which he happens to be, but might not have been, identical.[7] Aristotle's analysis provides alternative descriptions which can be substituted for each other without affecting the truth-value of a statement of cause. But his point is not merely linguistic, and it should not be construed primarily in these terms. In allowing that all the descriptions yield true statements of cause, Aristotle is committed to the view that causal contexts are referentially transparent; consistently, he adopts the essentialist stance that some ways of specifying the cause are prior to others. The bearing of essentialism on the way in which the reference of terms in causal contexts should be construed, has been emphasised in some recent discussion of this topic.[8]

Aristotle's focus is always on things, not just on words. To say that in addition to a builder, a man or a doctor is the cause of a house, is not simply using different words to express the same fact. Instead it introduces different things as the causes of the house; Aristotle's task is then to explain that these things are connected in ways which do not undermine the claim to completeness in the theory of the four causes. If we are to have an efficient cause of a house, what is essential is that it be caused by a builder. There may be other efficient causes also; but the central role of this item is not reduced. The requirement of referential transparency in causal contexts is met by declaring that all these various things—builder, doctor, and so on—really are causes. Once the connections among them have been analysed, we can rule out the suggestion, which would seriously undermine Aristotle's theory, that all these items must be given in order to produce a complete causal explanation.[9]

Necessity

Proposition (2) attributes universal necessity. To understand its significance for Aristotle's theory, we must say something about the way his predecessors regarded necessity. A curious feature of this is a tendency to oppose what happens from an intelligible cause and what happens by necessity.[10] Thus Plato in the *Timaeus* draws a grand contrast between those aspects of the workings of the universe which are fashioned by intelligence and what occurs through necessity; and although he does speak of necessity as a cause, he opposes its products to those things which we can find a reason for.[11] In viewing the matter in this way, Plato echoes a theme which had appeared among the Presocratics. An example is provided by the Atomists who expressed their rejection of any providence or plan in natural events by making everything the result of necessity.[12]

Some of Aristotle's remarks about causation and necessity reflect this background; indeed we owe our understanding of it in no small measure to the information he supplies. But there is a fundamental difference between his view and the views of the thinkers he comments on, which may be put simply: Aristotle makes necessity scientifically respectable. Unlike the earlier philosophers he does not assume that there is a difference in kind between what is necessary and what we can find rationally intelligible. The basis for this shift lies in his logical investigations. He recognises that success in argument and reasoning is marked by our ability and right to come up with statements flagged by the modal operators 'necessarily' and 'not possibly'. Further, a logical programme of this kind is a realisable ideal, as Aristotle is aware; for he brings one such programme to fruition with his detailed work on syllogistic inference. If success in reasoning and argument is the hallmark of rationality, we are at our most rational when we can produce statements which express necessities or impossibilities.[13]

Aristotle's predecessors had some grasp of this. As philosophers they were in the business of arguing, and they used modal terms to highlight their significant moves. Thus Plato in the *Phaedo* comments on a proof which has deduced the soul's independence of physical embodiment from the existence of certain objects which can be grasped only by reasoning: 'There is equal necessity that these should exist and that our souls exist before our birth.'[14] The necessity of a reasoned conclusion is linked here to a central thesis about the nature of our powers of reason. Earlier Parmenides had commented in similar vein: 'It must be that what is there to be spoken and thought should be.'[15] Clearly there are limits to the opposition, as these thinkers conceive it, between what is necessary and what is rationally intelligible. But Aristotle rightly perceives the need to correct the failure, in earlier accounts, to settle the relation between causation and necessity.

The apparent conflict between what we can bring about by deliberation and what happens of necessity is in fact a rather primitive strand in the antinomy of freedom and determinism. Some things are brought about by human agency, as a result of deliberation and choice; other things simply happen, independently of such deliberation. The language of necessity is easily applied to the latter kind of occurrence: 'what has to happen' rather than what happens through our agency but otherwise would not have done. Whatever we have no effect on is beyond our power to make otherwise. So there arises the idea that what comes about through deliberation is not necessary, and that the realm of the necessary includes all of what is beyond human agency.[16]

I call this line of thought primitive because while it stresses the role of human deliberation in certain occurrences, it exaggerates and simplifies the contrast between these cases and others where human agency is not involved. The problem of determinism begins to come into view; but just what the problem is, is far from clear. The focus becomes sharper when it is seen that both kinds of occurrence, which the original theory distinguished so sharply, are alike in being outcomes of particular antecedent factors; the same outcomes can be produced by human agency and can occur through 'natural necessity'. This suggests that there is a single framework of events, containing both human actions and natural occurrences, in which each kind of thing is brought about by its appropriate cause. Here we do have a problem of determinism. For what basis now is there for distinguishing deliberate actions from the occurrences of natural necessity?

Aristotle's views on change and causation are deeply influenced by the problems of determinism. As one would expect, this has bearing on the way he construes the claim of universal necessity in proposition (2). Aristotle makes much of a distinction between absolute and hypothetical necessity—that is, between what is simply necessary and what is necessary given certain conditions.[17] The distinction derives from reflection on ordinary usage of modal terms. When it is claimed that something is necessarily the case—for example, on surveying the wet ground one morning that it must have rained last night—we do not mean that the occurrence of the rain is unconditionally necessary but rather that there is a necessary connection between the currently observed state of the ground and some earlier rain: the former could not occur without the latter. It would be a mistake to understand the modal claim in accordance with its surface grammar. The force of 'must' is 'must, given such-and-such'; and the context of the utterance of the claim supplies the condition.

Determinism and Teleology

This linguistic thesis tells us nothing about the necessity or otherwise of what actually occurs. It is compatible with the view that everything is absolutely necessary, or that everything is relatively necessary, or some subtler variant. In fact Aristotle argues that while some features of the natural world are absolutely necessary, most are so only relatively; and the predominant form of relativity is relativity to some purpose or result to be realised later. So most of what actually happens *must* happen; and the justification of 'must' in this claim is of the form 'must, if such-and-such is to follow on'.[18]

We have already seen why Aristotle would be disposed to construe the hypothetical necessity of events in this forward-dependent way; so much is clear from the two arguments for teleology examined in Chapter 5. More ambitiously we are now engaged in deducing the correctness of this teleological approach from the theses just canvassed about causality, necessity and determinism. I shall start with Aristotle's most renowned rejection of determinism, the argument about tomorrow's sea-battle in *De Int*. 9.[19]

This discussion occurs in the course of a general logical investigation of the nature of contradiction. Aristotle is concerned to establish, for each general kind of statement, how they are to be paired as true or false. He investigates this question for singular, quantified and modal statements; and although the issues are shown to contain a number of difficulties, they turn out to be resoluble.[20] But with statements of future contingencies—such as 'there will be a sea-battle tomorrow' and 'there will not be a sea-battle tomorrow'—there appears an insuperable problem. For if either of these is true, then the fact of the future sea-battle is already determined, and has always been so; and this undermines the contingency of the event and of the statement describing it.

Aristotle's argument has always been the subject of much, frequently inconclusive discussion. He attributes a special status to statements about the future, as opposed to other times, but asserts that the law of the excluded middle applies to them as much as to other statements;[21] and it is most unclear how he can reconcile these two positions. His development of the fatalist position is based on two main points: any statement about the future is equivalent to statements about the present or the past, and the truth of a disjunction of the form *P or not P* is a function of the truth of at least one of its disjuncts.

It follows from the second point that a true disjunction about the future, given in the form of the law of the excluded middle, will contain a true statement as one of its disjuncts. It follows from the first point that this true statement is equivalent to a true statement about the present or past. Now the present and past are unalterable and, in this sense, necessary; the statement that E has happened is a statement about the necessity of the occurrence of E. The conclusion seems to follow that the equivalent statement about the futurity of E also expresses a necessary truth, if it expresses a truth at all.[22]

Aristotle rejects the conclusion of this argument, since he sees freedom of choice and moral responsibility as depending on the non-necessity of what is going to happen. But it is difficult to see where he makes any significant modification to the premises which generate the undesirable conclusion, or where he challenges the reasoning of the argument. The most likely key is a hint in his final comment on the relations of truth and falsity among the pairs of contradictory statements which express future contingencies:

> It is necessary that one limb of the contradiction be true or false, but not this one or that but as it chances,—and that one should be more true, but yet not be true or false. (19a36-9)

This is a hint, no more, that Aristotle might be prepared to introduce a special operator for future-tense statements which would enable him to distinguish between the truth of the statement that P will not be the case and the falsity of the statement that P will be the case. The recognition of such an operator would enable us to say, about any genuinely contingent future event, that it is not the case that it will occur, which is to be distinguished from saying that it is the case that it will not occur.[23] By this device it turns out that most statements about the future are false, since their contingency precludes the truth of statements of the form 'it is the case that E will/will not happen'. But it may be that in some cases, such as statements about what two plus two will equal tomorrow, it is the case that E will happen; here, exceptionally, there is a true statement about the future.

This proposal will preserve the law of the excluded middle for future contingents, which is one of Aristotle's aims in his analysis. On the other hand, he is concerned throughout the whole discussion of the *De Int.* to explicate and clarify the distinctions made by ordinary language; while these include the devices of quantification and modal operators, they do not extend to the kind of future-tense operator invoked in the preceding paragraph. So it is natural that most of what Aristotle says in the summary quoted above should reflect the telescoping in natural language of the distinctions we have just drawn. This explains the remark about one limb of the contradiction being 'more true'. The proposal cannot bear strict scrutiny in terms of the principle of the excluded middle, where truth and falsity must be all-or-nothing properties. But it may be acceptable on a loose interpretation of statements according to which P is true if it is not the case that P will not be true. Even if it is also not the case that P will be true, some estimate of the probabilities may sanction the verdict that P is more true than not-P is.

The speculations in our recent discussion, while inevitably inconclusive on a highly controversial matter, seem to be sanctioned by Aristotle's official comment on his analysis. Certainly our interpretation is in principle preferable to those which would dismiss his discussion as based on muddles about the logical relations between such versions of the law of the excluded middle as 'necessarily (P or not-P)' and 'necessarily-P or necessarily-not-P'.[24] At least it is clear—and on our interpretation of *De Int.* 9, more interestingly clear—that

Aristotle thinks that the most promising way to solve his difficulty lies in drawing a sharp distinction, of a modal kind, between statements about the future and statements about the present or past.

This analysis can now be connected with the earlier question of teleology and the direction of causation. If there is a fundamental difference between the future and other times in respect of necessity, this must have consequences for the tenability of a deterministic interpretation of events. Our original thesis (2) states that everything happens of necessity; but we know now that the necessity need not be absolute. It may be relative; perhaps what happens must happen, but only in the sense that its happening is an inevitable consequence of something else.

Aristotle reconciles his acceptance of necessity in scientific explanation and his rejection of determinism; he relies on the idea that the necessity of events is characteristically relative, not absolute.[25] What happens in the natural world is necessitated by its causes; but unless these too are necessary, the necessity of the effect will be only conditional. Aristotle was aware of the following modal theorem: if it is both necessary that if P, then Q, and it is necessary that P, then it is necessary that Q,[26] or in Lukasiewicz symbolism CKLCPQLPLQ.[27] He maintains that it is the business of science to establish conditional necessities of the form: it is necessary that if P, then Q (LCPQ). Such statements provide the causal links which must be discovered if we are to have a genuine explanation of why something happens. But how can we be sure that the necessity of an event is only of the conditional kind, so that we avoid any commitment to the absolute necessity which is characteristic of determinism? The modal theorem given above contains as one of its premisses a statement of the conditional necessity of a consequent in relation to its antecedent. This is not itself sufficient to establish the necessity of its conclusion Q. For this result to come about, the other premiss must be a statement of absolute necessity; we need LP as well as LCPQ.

From the problem of tomorrow's sea-battle and the debate about determinism, we have seen that what marks off statements about the future from those about other times is the lack of necessity in the former. So if the statement P in the premisses relates to the future, it will not be necessary; but if it relates to the present or past, it will be. In the former case we shall avoid the result that the conclusion Q is necessary, even though we accept the necessity of the connection between P and Q; but in the latter we see from the modal theorem that the necessity of Q cannot be avoided. Now teleological causation differs from mechanistic causation precisely in running from later to earlier time, not vice versa. While the distinction between earlier and later times is not the same as that between past and future, from the point of view of someone trying to explain some presently observed event, they amount to the same thing.

Suppose that we are confronted with some event requiring explanation. The options are either to follow the mechanists' strategy of looking for causes in the events which preceded our specimen event, or to prefer Aristotle's recommendation to look for the causes in the result to which the event is tending. If we adopt the former approach, the threat of determinism becomes insistent, since the cause of what necessitates our event is itself necessary. With Aristotle's teleological approach the item cited as the cause lies in the future, and so normally it will be contingent. There is no transmission of necessity from the cause to the event which it effects. Both theories of causation seek to establish necessary connections between antecedent and consequent, and thus the hypothetical necessity of the consequent. Only Aristotle's is able to restrict the necessity to the hypothetical kind, thereby avoiding a deterministic construction of events.

Chance and Causality

We have examined a major element in Aristotle's defence of the propositions (2) and (4) in the set given at the beginning of this chapter. His main justification for rejecting determinism is clear, and so also is his reason for maintaining that everything happens by necessity. But there is a further dialectical subtlety, arising from the interplay between propositions (1) and (3). It is natural for us to suppose, when Aristotle sets his face firmly against determinism, that he recognises the objective role of chance in events. Indeed thesis (3), which he certainly wants to uphold, seems to assert precisely this. How then can he also maintain (1)? For this proposition with its claim of a universal and comprehensive system of causal explanation, seems to leave no room for the operations of chance spoken of in (3).

Aristotle addresses the problem in *Physics* B4-5 immediately after his statement of the theory of four causes. He is concerned to combat any analysis of events and their causes which would show that chance events are excluded by his fourfold scheme.[28] If determinism is wrong—if some events do indeed occur by chance—it is very tempting to regard them as lying beyond the scope of explanation by one or more of the normal four causes.

A strongly indeterminist position, at the polar opposite from determinism in this debate, will seek to deny normal causes any role in the occurrence of chance events. Aristotle argues that this view of chance undermines itself. It was summed up in the description of chance as 'a cause which is obscure to human thinking', which he found among the current views.[29] The idea is that some things happen for reasons which we can understand, while others—those which we call chance events—happen for a reason which we cannot understand. Why then should the indeterminist not simply deny that the latter events happen for any reason at all? The difficulty with this position is that it is not proof against an advance in understanding which would render explicable what was previously obscure.[30] If such an advance occurs, earlier claims for inexplicability are defeated; and the mere possibility of its occurring always makes any such claim hollow and insecure. The problem is part of a more general one afflicting realism as it confronts verificationism. To say that certain truths are beyond the power of human discovery is either to say nothing definite or to give a hostage to fortune. Specify what the truths in question are, and you run the risk that later experience will succeed in verifying them.[31]

The indeterminist has reason to prefer his formulation of chance as playing a role which is causal, even though the causality is quite opaque to us. But Aristotle can reply that events which are caused by chance are not chance events. For it is essential to a chance event that it should be an unusual and unlikely development from the features of the situation preceding it; this condition would not be satisfied if there were some feature in the preceding state of affairs which regularly issued in a chance event. Yet on the proposal we are now considering, this is just how it would be. Chance events would be the regular outcome of those antecedent situations where chance operated as a cause. Proposition (3) could no longer be sustained.[32]

So the chance character of these events can only be preserved by some different account. The crucial element is the distinction, already considered, between the essential cause and other causes which are logically secondary to it. Aristotle's account of chance makes use of this idea in the context of teleology. If we accept teleology's central thesis that a cause of an event may lie in its future, that cause may have certain accidental properties; and if these are cited as the cause of the event, the event takes on a chance character, since that cause does not regularly produce that effect.

Aristotle's illustration of this thesis has caused some puzzlement; interpreted properly, it makes his point well enough.[33] An example of chance would be if someone, making one of his regular visits to the market, were to meet a long-lost debtor. The recovery of the debt could not have been foreseen, nor is such an outcome the regular result of the antecedents set out in the example. Here, Aristotle says, we have a case of chance operating as 'an accidental cause of the purposive kind in matters involving choice'.[34] This is a case of purposive action, with a sequence of events which are unusual enough to constitute chance; so it looks like a good candidate for the kind of analysis which Aristotle promises.

To see the point of the example it is necessary to identify correctly at which point the element of chance occurs. One might at first be inclined to say that the recovery of the debt is a matter of chance. If that were right, Aristotle's analysis would fail in this case; for we know nothing of what event, subsequent to the recovery, might be a final cause of *this*. On reflection it is not so much the recovery of the debt as its following on the regular visit to the market, that makes the sequence a plausible case of chance. In these circumstances what is chancy, and what we might feel inclined to invoke chance as explaining, is that particular occurrence of visiting the market.

There is a perfectly normal cause of the visit, and that is the purchase of goods. As is appropriate with purposive activity, the most illuminating kind of cause here is final; and we have a final cause which unproblematically produces our specimen effect, since the purchase of goods is the regular purpose and result of visiting the market. In the present case, unusually, the purchase of goods is the same event as meeting a debtor. The accidental identity means that meeting the debtor is a cause of this visit to the market, although only an accidental one.[35]

Aristotle here uses the idea which we encountered earlier in his defence of the completeness of his causal analysis, proposition (1) of our initial set. Accidental causal connections arise because any thing which is a cause is liable to have accidental properties. So what is picked out by such a property will also be a cause; this is how the doctor (who happens also to be a builder) comes to be a cause of the building of a house. Such examples of accidental causes do not weaken the claim that the account of the four kinds of cause is complete, because the items which are introduced as accidental causes are not things distinct from one of the four regular causes: the doctor is not a different person from the builder. This same idea is put to work in the account of chance. The meeting with a debtor is not the regular cause of visiting the market, and that is what makes this particular causal sequence a matter of chance. But it is not an event distinct from the buying of goods; and so the chance event is not caused by something distinct from what causes non-chance events. Chance is not a special cause; and the completeness of the theory of four causes is not compromised.[36]

If the notion of chance is illuminated by the notion of accidental cause, it remains to be considered why Aristotle particularly associates such causation with *final* causes. For it seems natural to see other types of cause as responsible for chance outcomes—the doctor as efficient cause of the house, or an ancient gravestone as the material cause of a stretch of garden path. To answer this we need simply to remind ourselves of the considerations adduced in the previous chapter in support of the programme of teleological explanation; there are good empirical and conceptual grounds for seeking principally to explain things by final causes. We should expect to understand chance events in the same teleological manner. They are deviations from a norm; as such they must exhibit similarities to as well as differences from the straightforward case. That is why the accidental causes we need to concentrate on in explaining chance are final causes.

The Solution

Much modern work on the analysis of events, actions and their causes is greatly influenced by the argument in Kant's second Analogy of Experience for a fundamental difference between events and enduring substances.[37] A leading example of analysis in this tradition is Davidson's treatment of change, in which the subject–predicate structure of statements which describe change is argued to be a misleading guide to the true logical structure of what has to be identified if change is to be understood correctly.[38] From such a perspective Aristotle's theorising on change may seem primitive. Although he does recognise a difference of category between predicates signifying substance and those signifying activity and passivity, this plays no major part in the theories which we have been considering here and in Chapter 5.

Aristotle's approach is important for his account of changing substance. Without it he could not establish so firmly his distance from a Platonic conception of substance as essentially immune to change. Kant appeals to the nature of causation to deduce the distinction between objects and events. Aristotle surveys both objects and events, without making much of the distinction between them, to clarify the nature of causation. His order of investigation seems the more intuitively natural, even though Kant produces the more spectacular argument. Until we may be moved by Kant's argument to stop doing so, we readily speak both of explosions and thunderstorms and of hammers and anvils as causes and effects, thereby revealing a non-discriminatory attitude to events and objects. That attitude is the basis of Aristotle's analysis.

We have followed a number of Aristotle's arguments through the complex terrain that was promised by the four propositions from which this chapter started. Initially they looked unpromising candidates for forming a consistent set. This has proved to be a misapprehension. The main contribution to the task of reconciliation has come from the theory of teleological causal analysis.

Consider again two of our original propositions: everything occurs of necessity, and some things occur by chance. These look irreconcilable; and on the standard view of forward-directed causation, they are. But the notion of backward causation, operating from future to past, provides an interpretation of each of these propositions which allows them to be both plausibly true and consistent with each other. The existence of chance events is shown to be an intrinsic, objective feature of what happens in the world. It is grounded in the distinction between essence and accident; so it is not at all correct to construe chance as simply a function of human ignorance. The same wish to avoid an obscurantist conception of events motivates Aristotle to maintain that all are necessary; but it is shown that this does not entail that each event, taken by itself, has to occur.

The particular devices which Aristotle uses to explain and justify these two propositions about necessity and chance, also serve to establish the fourth of our original propositions—that determinism is false. In the discussion of future contingency in *De Int*. 9 he treats the existence of human deliberation and responsibility as a basic datum, and in the discussion of chance in *Phys*. B4-5 he links the explanation of chance with the outcomes of choice. To this extent, in the debate over determinism Aristotle is to be placed firmly in the libertarian camp; it does not of course follow that he embraces the extreme libertarianism of denying the role of causal factors in chance events.

The main reason for denying that Aristotle's position approaches such an extreme lies in the first of our original propositions, the claim for completeness in his causal analysis. His opposition to determinism is most certainly not expressed in any reluctance to recognise the comprehensive role played by his fourfold causal scheme for the analysis of events, including those that happen by chance. No event, not even a chance event, is incapable of being wholly explained by the devices of this causal analysis. Moreover the leading factor in the causal analysis of chance is the final cause; and as we saw, the futurity of the final cause in relation to its effect is what makes it possible to reconcile the roles of necessity and chance in the generation of events.

So despite initial appearances to the contrary, the four propositions from which we started do indeed cohere. The careful examination of each shows how they complement each other so that a proper understanding of every one is required for each of the others. We have pursued this analysis of four propositions about causality and change in the larger context of an explanation and defence of teleology. The general form of the third, metaphysical argument for teleology is that only if teleology is true, is it possible to have a wholly adequate theory of the causes of all events. Aristotle's notion of causes operating from later to earlier time seems to come into deep conflict with the idea that causation runs with the direction of time. That is a problem for modern students of his theory; it was also a problem for Aristotle's own contemporaries. That is why he devotes so much attention to the refutation of the mechanistic theories of Empedocles and the Atomists.[39] But the metaphysical argument for teleology is designed to show us that the real problem lies with mechanist causal theory; it is these theorists, not Aristotle, who are unable to give an account of causality which does justice to the twin notions of necessity and chance.

The argument is notably dialectical in character. Aristotle's positive theory of causation is established more by showing up the inadequacies in alternative conceptions than by direct advocacy of his own conclusion. So we are first given an analysis presenting two different senses of 'necessary'; this by itself does not show which particular sense is the correct one for construing statements about the necessity of the events. Aristotle then goes on to show that one construal is to be preferred on the ground that the other leads to unacceptable paradox. More generally the main recommendation of a teleological theory of causation is the negative one that it provides the only coherent alternative to determinism.

The first two arguments do, of course, provide a positive case for teleology. But they are not by themselves strong enough to quell objections based on a mechanist view of causality. For that we need an examination of the weakness of this position; and the examination provides a more precise view of the nature of backward-directed causation. So we are given what is simultaneously a map of all the possible theoretical positions and an inducement to see one of them as more attractive than the others. The whole exercise well illustrates Aristotle's comment on the nature of philosophical investigation and progress: 'For those who wish to be free from difficulty it is profitable to go through the difficulties properly; for the subsequent freedom from difficulty is the resolution of the difficulties previously gone into, and those who are unaware of a knot cannot untie it.'[40]

Notes

1 As is happily acknowledged in the title, adapted from Hume, which J.L. Mackie gives his essay on causation, *The Cement of the Universe* (Oxford, 1974).

2 *Met*. Θ5, 1048a5-7; *Phys*. B9, 200b4-7; *Met*. Δ5, 1015a33-b6. These texts seem to tell against R.R.K. Sorabji, *Necessity, Cause and Blame* (London, 1980), pp.26-45, when he denies that Aristotle makes this connection betwen causation and necessity. Sorabji's book provides useful commentary on a number of issues discussed in the present chapter.

3 *Met*. E2, 1027a15-26; see the comments by C. Kirwan, *Aristotle's Metaphysics Books* Γ, Δ, E (Oxford, 1971), p.194.

4 There are some who have denied the appropriateness of even attempting to locate Aristotle within the debate over determinism; e.g. P. Huby, 'The First Discovery of the Freewill Problem', *Philosophy* 42 (1967), 353-62. I believe that this is to miss the essential continuity between Aristotle's discussion and later debate.

5 *De Int*. 9, 19a7-11.

6 *Phys*. B3, 195b12-16.

7 *Met*. E2, 1026b37-7a8; K8, 1065a28-30.

8 See D. Follesdal, 'Quantification into Causal Contexts', repr. in L. Linsky (ed.), *Reference and Modality* (Oxford, 1971), pp.52-62; G.E.M. Anscombe 'Causality and Extensionality', repr. in *Collected Philosophical Papers* vol.2 (Oxford, 1981), pp.173-9.

9 *Phys*. B3, 195b21-28.

10 See W.K.C. Guthrie, *A History of Greek Philosophy*, vol.2 (Cambridge, 1965), pp.414-19.

11 *Timaeus* 47e-8a.

12 See G.S. Kirk, J.E. Raven, M. Schofield (eds.), *The Presocratic Philosophers* (Cambridge, 1983), pp.418-20.

13 The theory of necessary consequence is developed in *Prior Analytics* esp. A4-6. There is also a specialised section on *modal* inference (*An. Pr*. A8-22) which is less satisfactorily worked out. Although the programme of scientific argument expounded in the *Posterior Analytics* appears to depend on both these elements, in fact its main support comes from the first, the general theory of necessary consequence. For the absorption of these logical ideas into his philosophical analysis of necessity, see *Met*. Δ5, 1015b6-9.

14 *Phaedo* 76e5-6.

15 Fr. 6.1.

[16] For some discussion of this theme, see H. Lloyd-Jones, *The Justice of Zeus* (California, 1971), p.106.
[17] *P.A.* A1, 639b21-40a9; *G.C.* B11, 337b15-29.
[18] *Phys.* B9, 199b34-200a7, 200a24-7.
[19] The most thorough and careful commentary on this passage is by J.L. Ackrill, *Aristotle's Categories and De Interpretatione* (Oxford, 1963), pp.132-42. Two further contributions which I have found useful, are G.E.M. Anscombe, 'Aristotle and the Sea Battle', repr. in J.M.E. Moravcsik (ed.) *Aristotle: A Collection of Critical Essays* (New York, 1967), pp.15-33, and S.R.L. Clark, *Aristotle's Man* (Oxford, 1975), pp.118-22.
[20] *De Int.* 7, 17b37-18a7; 12, 21b17-32.
[21] *De Int.* 9, 19a29-32.
[22] *De Int.* 9, 18b9-15. We have here an application of the argument from truth-value links between statements involving different times; the form of argument may have been suggested by Plato *Parmenides* 151e-3b.
[23] Another passage which suggests this is *G.C.* B11, 337b3-7, where Aristotle distinguishes what *will be* so—of which it is at some time true that it *is* so—and what is *going to* be so, where there is no corresponding truth-value link to a present tense statement.
[24] Elsewhere Aristotle makes these scope distinctions quite satisfactorily; see Chapter 5, pp.96-7 above.
[25] See n. 18 above; and we can now add *De Int.* 9, 19a23-6.
[26] *An. Pr.* A15, 34a22-4.
[27] J. Lukasiewicz, *Aristotle's Syllogistic from the Standpoint of Modern Formal Logic* (Oxford, 1957), pp.138-40. My formulation of the principle differs slightly from his in order to highlight the attributions of necessity in the antecedent; the point does not affect the logic.
[28] *Phys.* B4, 196a1-14.
[29] *Phys.* B4, 196b6.
[30] Cf. *Met.* A3, 984b8-18.
[31] This is Berkeley's basic argument against a reality which is independent of the mind (*Principles of Human Knowledge* Part 1, 22-4; *Three Dialogues between Hylas and Philonous* I, 200); see my 'Berkeley on Conceiving the Unconceived', *Irish Philosophical Journal* 2 (1985), 79-93. For further moves in this debate, see the realist argument in W.D. Hart, 'The Epistemology of Abstract Objects', *Aristotelian Society Supplementary Volume* 53 (1979), p.156.
[32] *Phys.* B5, 196b10-13; cf. *An. Post.* A30.
[33] *Phys.* B5, 196b29-7a6; cf. B4, 196a3-5. For the best interpretation, see W. Charlton, *Aristotle's Physics I,II* (Oxford, 1970) pp.107-8.
[34] *Phys.* B5, 197a5-6.
[35] For the notion of accidental identity in Aristotle, cf. *Top.* A7, 103a29-31; *Met.* Δ9, 1017b27-33.
[36] *Phys.* B5, 197a12-17; B6, 198a5-13.
[37] *Critique of Pure Reason* A195-8/B240-3.
[38] D. Davidson, 'The Logical Form of Action Sentences', and 'Events as Particulars', in *Essays on Actions and Events* (Oxford, 1980), pp.105-48, 181-7.

[39] *Phys*. B8, 198b10-36; *P.A*. A1, 640b5-1a18.
[40] *Met*. B1, 995a27-30.

CHAPTER 7

Philosophy of Psychology

The subject of this chapter is Aristotle's philosophy of mind. Its topic is mind and thought. There are numerous indications in the work *De Anima* that his focus of interest is rather different, and commentators have sounded very reasonable cautions against regarding his work as belonging to the same enterprise as post-Cartesian philosophy of mind.[1] For all that, the nature of the human mind and its relation to everything else are his theme.

De Anima, the work which we shall examine, means 'On the Soul'. As we saw in Chapter 2, the title promises discussion of what is essential to life[2]—human life mainly, since it is the human kind of soul which forms Aristotle's principal concern. So his official topic extends beyond the mind and its operations, since humans do more than think; still, his discussion is firmly centred on this most fundamental of human life-functions.

If there is a significant restriction in Aristotle's approach in the *De Anima*, it is the exclusion of considerations which go beyond the *natural* features of persons. Individual personal identity consists in large part of character and self-consciousness, and these are induced by habituation, training and teaching.[3] Aristotle provides argument for regarding these factors as essentially lying beyond the province of the philosophy of nature, including human nature. When they have been removed, what is left for natural philosophy is theorising which assigns to the mind a central position in the natural scheme of things, while eschewing any tendency to idealism.

We shall concentrate on two large problems which dominate the *De Anima*: these are the unity of the person, and the relation between the person, especially the consciousness, and the external world. The discussion of the first problem provides a classic example of Aristotle's dialectical practice of steering a middle course between two extremes which seem to exhaust the possibilities. As we saw earlier, he notes that there are two leading views—the materialism which identifies a person with his body, and the dualism which sees each person as a conjunction of the two substances of body and soul. Aristotle applies his general analysis of the relation between matter and form in natural substances in order to stake out a third view of personal identity. A person is only one substance, but this substance is the soul, rather than the body as in materialist monism. Since the soul is defined as the form of a natural body, this account of the unity of the person is straightforward if the ontological results of Chapter 4 are understood.[4] What remains to be done, to give credibility to this particular claim for unity between form and matter in a substance, is to show how the form—the soul—can be a principle of unity.

The Unity of the Person

Aristotle insists against the dualist that thought and mind alone do not constitute the form of a living human body. The materialist is equally wrong in maintaining that every life-function of the body must be performed by a particular bodily organ or limb. Aristotle notes several times that thinking is an exception to the general strategic requirement of including bodily factors in the explanation of what it is to live in a certain way.[5] But the full significance of this has not, I think, been adequately grasped by students of his account.

Aristotle maintains that the concept of soul is what we may term a *serial* concept. Other examples of such concepts are those of number and dimensionality; and since these examples are more accessible, let us start with them. It is wrong to construe the individual numbers or the dimensions of shape simply as coordinate items falling under an overall general concept. This construction not only obscures the fact that the individuals do occur in the definite order given by the series; it also misinterprets the role of the general concept in establishing the serial order. Each particular number is differentiated from any other number by some particular number; 5, for example, is differentiated from 3 by 2.[6] Similarly, though perhaps less obviously, what distinguishes a particular shape from another—say, a triangle from a point—are just those items—a point, a line—which themselves belong within the ordered series of dimensions of shape.[7] The general concepts of number or shape as such play no part in these analyses.

Aristotle's fullest explanation of the notion of a serial concept occurs through such mathematical examples; but he also uses it in non-mathematical cases. One of the most striking cases is in the analysis of what it is to be a citizen member of the different systems of political constitution.[8] His reason for applying it to the concept of soul is that the souls of different varieties of living creature exhibit the same kinds of mutual entailment that are found with other serially ordered items. Just as 6 presupposes 5, and a line presupposes a point, so the life of a creature that can alter its location presupposes a life which possesses the faculty of nutrition.

This claim about the soul has two main aspects, one empirical and the other conceptual. It is a matter of empirical fact that all creatures with locomotive power also have the faculty of nutrition, whereas the converse is not so—witness the case of plants. As a matter of conceptual necessity the ability to engage in locomotion requires the sort of physical body—more particularly, parts such as legs and kidneys—which possesses the power of nutrition.[9] In the case which interests us most, that of the human being, the power of thought presupposes all the faculties possessed by more elementary forms of life, but not conversely; the human soul comes later in the series than the souls of non-human animals and plants.[10]

This serial analysis of souls demonstrates that a general concept of soul is redundant. One particular item in the series is distinguished from another by an item which also appears in the series. Aristotle does not work out this idea explicitly for the case of soul. But we may presume, by analogy with the case of numbers, that what he has in mind is this: a worm differs from a plant by the faculty of locomotion. We know that the faculty of locomotion does not occur in isolation from that of nutrition; that is why the former follows after the latter in the series. So the distinction between the locomotive soul and the nutritive soul will be well founded only if the first is understood in some sense to incorporate the second. The same thing happens in the case of numbers; the larger numbers later in the series incorporate their smaller predecessors, as is taught by good philosophy of arithmetic.[11]

This is somewhat abstract; and this indeed is how Aristotle presents it. But it points to an idea which is of great importance for the issue of personal identity. In his view, what distinguishes the human soul from that of any other living creature is the power of thought.[12] This power must somehow incorporate each of the other powers which may be found in isolation in some living creature more simple than the human; otherwise Aristotle will be wrong in his claim that soul is a serial concept. It follows that thought is involved in every capacity of human life and that no aspect of human life-function will be adequately understood if the element of intelligence is ignored.

Aristotle's discussions of the varieties of human soul range from an examination of digestion and nutrition to an analysis of thought; and perception is taken in along the way. His treatment of all these topics is very similar; in particular, he consistently uses the idea that the change in question involves the soul assimilating something previously external to it. When a person either digests or thinks something, he becomes similar to the digested or the thought object, where each was distinguishable from the subject before the experience;[13] and these processes of assimilation are the realisations of specific capacities which characterise this mode of life. There is a close parallel between what might otherwise be supposed to be two very different functions.

It is, of course, only a parallel. Aristotle in no way suggests that one of the functions somehow reduces to the other, so that digestion becomes an essentially conscious activity, or thinking becomes as purely physiological as digestion. One of his problems in the analysis of perception is to explain how we perceive that we perceive;[14] and a parallel problem arises with thought. But there is nothing analogous to this reflexivity in the phenomena of nutrition. The notion of a serial concept should not make us confuse different members of the series, but it should lead us to expect that the analysis of an earlier member of the series will bring effective illumination to a later member. So it is in the present case. The analyses of perception and thought depend heavily on the discussion of faculties, such as nutrition and locomotion, which humans share with more elementary forms of life. Aristotle's approach appears to suggest a closer connection between human life and bovine or feline life than is found in other theories; but caution is needed here. The comparison with non-human life indicates that a comprehensive account of the human soul should include those respects in which it approximates to other forms. Even so, human life—or any other distinct form of life—is special through and through.

As in so many other cases which we have examined, Aristotle's position can best be appreciated by contrasting it with simpler views on the particular topic; these simple views represent the extremes which Aristotle is at pains to avoid. The question here is what precisely is the relation between human and other forms of life, and the problem is that there appears to be a partial overlap between them. In the face of this, one of two reactions is likely: either we can concentrate on the features which are peculiar to human life, particularly the exercise of thought, and ignore those which humans share with non-humans, or we can divide up the concept of a human person so that a person effectively becomes the sum of the parts which are his particular faculties.

The first of these reactions is found in Plato's analysis of persons, especially the *Phaedo*; but it is prefigured in some earlier philosophy of Pythagorean tendency.[15] The second reaction, known currently as homunculus-theory,[16] can easily be attributed to Aristotle. But our examination of the way in which the human soul is located in a larger series of souls, shows that such a fragmentation of the human soul does not correspond to his idea. The number 5 is wholly distinct from the number 4, even though their positions in the number series make it seem that there is a four-fifths overlap between them. Similarly, one can suppose that there is no significant difference between human and non-human forms of faculties, such as nutrition and locomotion, which appear to be found in both humans and other animals.[17] This is the mistake which Aristotle corrects by applying the notion of a series to the analysis of the soul.

In order to recognise the unity of the human person we must be alert to how it is connected with other forms of life, but not so as to compromise the nature of a person as a unified and wholly distinct kind of living creature. It follows that Plato was right to concentrate on the most distinctive human faculty—thought—even though he was wrong to dismiss the other faculties as essentially sub-human. Aristotle, by contrast, finds in the nature of thought the key to the analysis of all human faculties.

The interpretation I am offering reverses a common verdict on Aristotle's psychology.[18] The more usual interpretation follows the order of Aristotle's exposition; psychological phenomena are treated as closely parallel to physical and physiological processes. But this is an uncritical reading of his whole theory about how a human being interacts with the rest of the world. Aristotle's work in ethics takes its start from the rationality of persons and extends this insight to analyse areas of human action where more than just thought is involved. In his psychology, on the other hand, the natural world provides the setting for his examination of the human person; and he considers its interaction with other natural objects. From this perspective, thought is only one component in a complex of natural processes; for reasons deriving from his serial analysis of living creatures, Aristotle examines it last. But a correct reading of his theory should give greater prominence to thought.

Thought and Things

One problem recurs through Aristotle's entire discussion of human life-functions. Every one of them can be understood in terms both of its content and the external objects to which it relates; indeed, in any adequate account both elements must be recognised. Thinking contains thoughts, appetite desires, and nutrition foods. Internal objects like these give the content of each individual faculty as it is exercised: as a matter of logic, they are necessary for the faculties to operate at all. At the same time these faculties are what relate us to the outside world. So there must be more to be said about what we think, desire, or digest than is supplied by the first, purely logical line of analysis.

Thinking is the most comprehensive of the ways in which we interact with the world.[19] We are restricted in what we digest and even, to a much lesser extent, in what we perceive. But there is nothing which we cannot think. Idealists have seen this as support for their contention that reality is created by the mind; but this is not Aristotle's approach. He is interested in discovering what it is about reality and the mind that makes the universality of thought possible. The answer lies in the notion of form. Everything has a form, which makes it possible for everything to be thought. The mind itself has no intrinsic nature; it is a pure potentiality and only acquires actual existence when actually thinking. That is why there is no restriction on what the mind can think.[20]

If it were like a sense, with a sense organ of some definite nature, the mind's capacity to think anything would be limited. The nature of the organ would be incompatible with the contents of certain thoughts and so would exclude them, in the same way that the nature of perceptual or digestive organs makes some objects impossible for them to perceive or to digest. An essential feature of Aristotle's theory of the mind is, therefore, that thinking should not require the operation of any physical part.[21] Even when we are able to interact with external objects apart from by thinking them, thought is still a distinctive mode of interaction; and this too needs to be explained. What is special about our thinking something, as opposed to perceiving or eating it, is that we are affected only by its form, not by its matter.[22] As we saw in Chapter 4, form is the structure which makes possible the independent existence of a substance. We rejected the interpretation which made form universal, since it is precisely by virtue of its form that each substance possesses existence as a particular thing.[23] When Aristotle says here in the *De Anima* that the objects of thought are forms, he is evidently referring to the role of form in making particular things *intelligible*.

The mind is nothing actual until it thinks. It then takes on the form of what it thinks. This theory of mental activity represents Aristotle's contribution to a line of thought which later was to be associated with the concept of intentionality, and philosophers like Aquinas and Brentano made great use of his insights.[24] The actual condition of a mind engaged in thinking is defined by the content of the thought; and the content is identical with the form of the external object of the thought. This is Aristotle's explanation of the mind's capacity to understand the whole of external reality; it is entirely consistent with his account of the processes of change in the natural world.

In his discussion of thinking Aristotle makes much use of the thesis that the mind and its objects are identical.[25] As we shall see in Chapter 10, this thesis has significant consequences outside the particular discipline of psychology; so it is important to understand its basis in his general psychological theory. Aristotle poses the problem of our relation to the external world in a deliberately archaic form, which is nonetheless true to his naturalistic conception of the kind of explanation appropriate to psychology.

A psychological event is a change. Must the items involved in the change be like or unlike each other? A ready example of a kind of natural change which raises this problem is mixture: for mixture to occur, should the ingredients be like or unlike? Since psychological events, naturalistically conceived, are mixtures between the subject and the external world, the question of similarity and dissimilarity between the ingredients arises here too.[26]

Earlier theorists about perception were worried by this very question. Some argued that the elements in this relation—the perceiver and the perceived—were similar, and some that they were dissimilar. Aristotle accepts the problem as stated in these terms, and subjects it to a classic dialectical resolution. Both parties are right and both are wrong. To reconcile them, a distinction which both have missed must be drawn between potentiality and actuality. Just as the ingredients in a mixture are actually different before the mixture, although potentially the same, so the factors which are joined in a perception are actually different but potentially the same. The activity of perception converts this potentiality to actuality, so that when someone actually perceives something, the perceiver takes on the same character as what is perceived.[27]

Aristotle argues that the language of perception is systematically ambiguous between the two senses of potentiality and actuality. Such terms as 'sight', 'hearing', 'sound', 'taste', in Greek as in English, can refer both to the capacity for involvement in perception and to actual perceptions themselves.[28] Aristotle notes a reformist proposal to separate the terminology for the two modes of perception; but he observes that this would require considerable innovation and coinage of new terms.[29] In fact, it is more instructive to stick with the relatively impoverished terminology of ordinary language and to reflect on the conceptual confusion which this can engender; the situation is similar to the one encountered in the analysis of 'ambition' in Chapter 2.

Here it is useful to note a further feature of the language of perception. This time English usage differs from Greek; and when we compare and contrast the two, we get on the track of the point which Aristotle's analysis reveals. English sometimes uses the same terms to refer both to the perceived object and to the perception. The double use of a term such as 'smell' or 'taste' reflects perfectly what Aristotle argues to be the facts of the matter as far as the actualities are concerned; since the actuality of the sense of taste and what is tasted are one and the same, the identity is accurately indicated by the use of the single term. But the situation is different with the corresponding potentialities; and here a more accurate indication of the facts is available through the Greek habit of using distinct terms for what perceives and what is perceived—for example, 'hearing' and 'sound'.[30]

Aristotle maintains that it was the failure to draw the distinctions between potentiality and actuality that led earlier theorists of perception into error. They supposed that nothing could be coloured independently of sight, nor flavoured without taste. About this he says:'In a way they spoke correctly, but also in a way not. For perception and what is perceived are so spoken of in a double sense—potentially and actually; and with the former the result is as they said, but not with the latter. They spoke simply about what is not so spoken of simply.'[31]

These philosophers were led into a version of subjective phenomenalism through lack of the distinction between potentiality and actuality. They overlooked the fact that perceivers retain their capacity for perception, even in the absence of anything perceived (either actually or potentially). More obviously still, things would remain perceptible even if there were nobody (again in either sense) to perceive them. A converse mistake would be made by extreme realists taking the view that the existence of the perceiver and the perceptible are wholly independent of each other. If this were right, there would be no sense at all in which the existence of colours or flavours logically required the existence of creatures with vision or taste. Aristotle insists that the actual existence of something perceived is indistinguishable from the actual perception of it; in this way he marks his distance from the realist account of the relation between perceivers and the world.

The account of thought and its object exactly parallels this account of perception; the distinction between actuality and potentiality is put to the same use in characterising both the dependence and the independence of the mind and what it thinks. Here again the use of the word 'thought' to describe both the activity of the mind and the nature of what it contemplates provides a confirmation from ordinary language of a main part of Aristotle's thesis.[32] We can now return to our earlier problem about the connection between the contents of thought and the external world of objects. Aristotle's analysis of the actuality and potentiality of thought yields the following conclusion. The object of thought is independent of thought, to the extent that its potentiality for being thought does not rely on the existence of a thinking mind; but when it is actually thought, it becomes the content of the mind that thinks it. The actualisation of the potentiality for being thought represents a shift in status from object to content. This is not idealism; the content of the thought retains the capacity for existing apart from the mind—that is, as an external object.

Aristotle argues that the account of perception and thought should run in parallel. The account of perception comes first in his order of exposition; but the general psychological thesis fits thought more precisely than perception, so that thought becomes the logically prior phenomenon. The reason is that thought does not employ a bodily organ and so is not restricted, as perception is, in its ability to assimilate external objects into contents of the soul. This recalls an earlier point about the contrast between the unrestrictedness of thought and the more limited powers of the other psychological faculties. In terms of the present analysis of the relation between contents and objects, the limitation of the non-intellectual faculties is that they cannot convert every object into a content. Some objects are imperceptible and some are indigestible, but none is unthinkable.[33]

In the case of thought the occurrence of causal contact guarantees the production of the appropriate intentionality when we encounter some part of the world. It is the same mode of causal contact that we get with the other psychological faculties; but with them the causal ingredients do not always succeed in producing the best result. The unvarying success of thought, as contrasted with the partial success of the other faculties in securing interaction between the soul and the world, is the reason for assigning this faculty logical priority. This is why its analysis forms the basis of Aristotle's theory of personal identity, and why his psychology, even in terms of his own generous conception of that enterprise, is a philosophy of mind.

The Mind and the Person

Modern philosophy of mind is much occupied with the problem of reconciling the facts of conscious experience with the multifarious nature of our causal interaction with the world. The former might be quite different in character from the latter; yet surely both must be recognised in any adequate theory of the mind. Sometimes the two facets of the data are labelled as the first-person perspective and third-person perspective.[34] Yet this is to recognise a problem, not to solve it.

Aristotle's theory should be evaluated in the context of this methodological problem. On the one hand, he consistently adopts the approach of the natural philosopher in his examination of psychology. The phenomena, including those of perception and thought, are analysed from the outside as processes of causal interaction between a person and his environment. This way we have the third-person approach. On the other hand, the content of Aristotle's analysis presents the result of the interaction as an internalising of the objects of our psychological processes. Sound becomes heard sound; an object becomes the thought of that object. Thus an account of the world which we experience is also an account of what it is to experience that world. So in this way we have a first-person approach to psychological phenomena.[35]

We set out to examine Aristotle's handling of two main problems in his psychology—the unity of the person, and the relation between the person and the rest of the world. The key to both lies in the nature of thought. The case of the relation between thinking and its object provides a model for the analysis of the relations of the other psychological faculties to their objects; the relation is seen in purer and more paradigmatic form with thought than with the other faculties. Thought is also the factor that unifies a person, diverse and complex though his range of psychological faculties may be. This is the import of Aristotle's serial analysis of the varieties of living creature. The last member of the series incorporates all the earlier members. They can exist apart from it, but in the last member they are subsumed under it. So while there are living creatures which digest without perceiving, or which perceive without thinking, with human beings these other functions do not occur independently of thinking. That is why it is right to regard Aristotle's theory of the soul as an exercise in the philosophy of mind.

The tradition from which Aristotle set out contained two leading strands. First, there was the emphasis on the nature and independence of the mind. Those like Plato who took this view, proceeded in the direction of dualism, so that they came to regard the study of the natural body and its processes as irrelevant to the proper understanding of the person.[36] Secondly, there were those who emphasised the importance of bodily attributes in the lives of human beings. These thinkers, represented by many of the Presocratics as well as by medical writers, treated human life as a natural phenomenon, to be studied through the same methods and concepts as the rest of the natural world.

Aristotle's work is a reconciliation of these two strands. He recognises the importance of both the mind and the body, and he rejects the dualistic way of understanding the human being which separates the two. He is not a materialist; for he does not provide any physical basis for the mind. But he does not go to the other extreme of divorcing the mind altogether from the body. His account alone explains how mind and body go together to make one complete person. The person thus understood belongs to the complex causal network of the physical world; and it is specifically by virtue of the relation of consciousness that he so belongs. In Aristotle's analysis, mind serves not to remove human nature from the physical world, but to secure its proper place within it.

Notes

1 W.I. Matson, 'Why isn't the mind–body problem ancient?', in P.K. Feyerabend and G. Maxwell (eds.), *Mind, Matter, and Method* (Minneapolis, 1966), pp.92-102; R.R.K. Sorabji, 'Body and Soul in Aristotle', *Philosophy* 49 (1974), 63-89. A view closer to the one I shall advance is found in J. Barnes, 'Aristotle's Concept of Mind', *Proceedings of the Aristotelian Society* 72 (1971–72), 101-14.

2 Chapter 2, pp.29-34 above.

3 So the appropriate place for discussing them is in studies whose aim is practical or result-oriented rather than simply directed at knowledge; cf. *E.N.* B1, 1103a18-26, and for the importance of the *Rhetoric* in the analysis of emotion W.W. Fortenbaugh, 'Aristotle's Rhetoric on Emotions', *Archiv für Geschichte der Philosophie* 52 (1970), 40-70.

4 *De An.* B1, 412a19-20; cf. Chapter 4, pp.75-8 above.

5 *De An.* A1, 403a6-8; Γ4, 429b3-5; Γ5, 430a17-18; *G.A.* B3, 736b28-9.

6 *Met.* B3, 999a6-9; *E.E.* A8, 1218a2-8. I have followed the interpretation of W.D. Ross, *Aristotle's Metaphysics*, vol. 1 (Oxford, 1924), p.237.

7 *De An.* B3, 414b28-31.

8 *Pol.* Γ1, 1275a33-b3. See Chapter 9, pp.161-2 below.

9 *De An.* B3, 415a1-13; cf. Γ3, 428a8-11.

10 *De An.* A2, 404b1-6; B3, 415a7-10.

11 For the definitional connections between the members of a series, cf. *Top.* Z4, 141b3-22; *Met.* M2, 1077a26-b4. These passages recognise a sense in which later members of the series are conceptually prior to earlier.

12 This is most extensively argued in *E.N.* A13, 1102a23-8, 1103a1-7; but although Aristotle refers there to 'popular' psychological works, what he says is quite consistent with the *De Anima*.

13 *De An.* B4, 416b3-9; Γ4, 429a15-29.

14 *De An.* Γ2, 425b12-25.

15 See Chapter 2, p.32 above.

16 Cf. D.C. Dennett, *Brainstorms* (Harvester, 1978), pp.122-4.

17 *De An.* Γ10, 433a9-12.

18 See D.W. Hamlyn, *Aristotle's De Anima, Books II and III* (Oxford, 1968), p.135.

19 *De An.* Γ4, 429a18-20, b1-4.

20 *De An.* Γ4, 429a27-9; Γ5, 430a10-15. In these chapters Aristotle draws a distinction, which has been much discussed, between the mind in its creative and its receptive aspects. I agree with Hamlyn, *op. cit.*, p.140 that the basis of the distinction lies in metaphysical considerations, and that it is not important for the philosophy of mind.

21 *De An.* Γ4, 429a20-7.

22 *De An.* Γ4, 429b10-22; and for the importance of form in thought, cf. Γ8, 431b28-2a6. *De An.* B12, 424a18-24 also proposes form as the object of perception, but restricts this to the forms of certain qualities (cf. B6, 418a11-16); thought, not perception, is needed to grasp the form of most things.

23 Chapter 4, pp.75-8 above.

24 See A. Marras, 'Scholastic Roots of Brentano's Concept of Intentionality', in L.L. McAlister (ed.), *The Philosophy of Brentano* (London, 1976), pp.128-39; Barnes, *op. cit.* (n.1 above).

25 *De An.* Γ4, 430a2-9; cf. Γ8, 431b21-3.

26 *De An.* Γ4, 429b22-9; cf. Chapter 5, pp.98-9 above.

27 *De An.* Γ2, 425b26-6a26.

28 *De An.* Γ2, 426a6-9.

29 *De An.* Γ2, 426a1, 11-15.

30 Aristotle is careful to keep the subjective and objective vocabulary distinct, even in a case like that of smell (*De An.* B10) where this involves some strain. R.D. Hicks, *Aristotle De Anima* (Cambridge, 1907), p.391 rather misleadingly suggests that Aristotle is less scrupulous in this matter than in fact he is.

31 *De An.* Γ2, 426a22-6.

32 A striking example of the ambiguity of the Greek word (*noēma*) is provided by Plato *Parmenides* 132b-c. Once again Aristotle is scrupulous in his terminology; but for the close connection between thought as psychological activity and as content, see *De An.* A3, 407a7; Γ6, 430a26-8.

33 *De An.* B4, 416a21-27; B12, 424a28-32; Γ4, 429b1-5.

34 See C. McGinn, *The Character of Mind* (Oxford, 1982), pp.6-7, 19-21; cf. T. Nagel, 'Subjective and Objective', repr. in *Mortal Questions* (Cambridge, 1979), pp.196-213.

35 *De An.* Γ8, 431b28-2a6.

36 This is the view of the *Phaedo* and the *Republic* rather than the *Timaeus*; but even in the latter work there is a strong dichotomy between the mind and the body (cf. 69c-e).

CHAPTER 8

Ethics

The *Nicomachean Ethics* has exercised a more direct and thorough influence on current philosophy than any other work of Aristotle. It is a central document in moral philosophy—for some philosophers, the best single contribution to their subject. Because of the range of its conceptual distinctions and its sophistication of method, it can function as an exemplary introduction to philosophy in general.

Some contemporary philosophers would say that Aristotle's work on ethics is the ancestor of two, not one, of the present branches of philosophy.[1] Not only does it set the agenda for much subsequent speculation in ethics; it also defines important issues in the philosophy of action which only recently have come to prominence. Action is the general topic in Aristotle's ethical theory.[2] He investigates problems in the valuation of actions, the subject of ethics; but he also considers more general issues about how action is based in thought and desire. Since these issues often lack the normative features of ethical questions, they have appeared properly to belong to a separate department of philosophical enquiry.

This modern reading of Aristotle well reflects the range of topics covered in his work on ethics. But its separation of normative and non-normative aspects of the analysis of action is mistaken. An accurate view of Aristotle's overall aim, and of the philosophical background, carries useful lessons for contemporary investigations which trace their ancestry back to the *Nicomachean Ethics*.[3]

Compared with the leading alternatives, such as Kantianism or Utilitarianism, the most distinctive note of Aristotle's ethical thought is the importance it places on *human character.* For the Utilitarians the central issue in ethics is what should be done or what state of affairs should prevail; for Kant, it is what intention should motivate our action. But the focus of Aristotle's interest is best defined by the question: What sort of person should I be?[4] Our word 'ethics' is transliterated from a Greek word meaning 'pertaining to character'. Virtue and vice of character are literally 'ethical virtue and vice' in his terminology; and the linguistic pedigree of 'moral virtue and vice' has similar Latin origins.

The Nature of Value: Plato and Aristotle

Aristotle does not simply assume that attention to character provides the correct approach. He argues for this position, and we shall consider how the argument works. First, let us look at the views of Plato and Socrates on the nature and study of value. They are more alien to modern ears than anything in Aristotle; but they influenced him considerably.

Both thinkers, in different ways, made the study of value the foundation of a true grasp of reality. With Socrates this took the form of a relatively unreflective sense that the most revealing questions to pursue about each thing were: what is the point of it, and under what conditions does it function best? No pretension to expertise could be accepted if it did not successfully address these questions.[5] Plato systematised this approach and argued that it should be extended beyond any narrow conception of the human sphere. His key principle in the scheme of reality is the Form of the Good; and the highest state of scientific knowledge is the synoptic vision of dialectic which understands each item in terms of its dependence on this principle.[6]

Although much of this theorising is visionary and programmatic, there are two reasons why it should be taken into account in assessing Aristotle's work. First, it provides the context for his efforts to circumscribe the area of value that is proper to ethics. As we shall see, both in general intention and in detail, Aristotle's argument here is firmly directed against Plato's conception of a value that transcends the human sphere. Secondly, a notable feature of the Socratic/Platonic background is its intellectualism. One of Socrates' leading theses is that knowledge of goodness is a necessary and sufficient condition of the good life; Plato's *Protagoras* presents arguments for this conclusion in the more colourful guise of the three Socratic 'paradoxes' that virtue is single, virtue is knowledge, and no one does wrong deliberately.[7]

Because Plato and Socrates are so convinced of the crucial role which knowledge of value plays in the pursuit of the good life, they are not simply uncompromising objectivists about value; they also regard value as the key to objective knowledge in general. Their views on knowledge and value reinforce each other in the converse order. If goodness is the fundamental principle in the reality of things, it is natural to suppose that the main ingredient in the good life is intellectual; for understanding is the only relation in which we stand to the great majority of things.

These ideas of Socrates and Plato on value may seem outlandish to modern ears. We are not disposed to accept the central place accorded to value in their account of objective scientific knowledge; and many today would question the importance given to the intellect in their analysis of human action, believing that factors such as will and emotions carry at least as much weight and, in the view of some philosophers following Hume, much more. If Plato's position represents one extreme and the modern opposition the other, Aristotle characteristically steers a middle way.

The best moral philosophy does not start from any explicit distinction between moral and other forms of value. Rather its strategy is to pursue criteria which will capture what is most fundamentally valued—the most valuable among values—and to show that the results of applying these criteria correspond to our pre-analytic intuitions about what is good and bad. The merit of the strategy is that it holds out the prospect of a direct answer to the very basic question: Why should we be moral?[8]

Aristotle's approach is to be understood in this context. His main criterion is self-sufficiency; the values we seek are those about which it does not make sense to ask for further justification. Any candidate for supreme value, such as pleasure or wealth, that is subject to further valuation in other terms, will fail this criterion, since there will arise the further question of whether they are good or bad examples of their kind. They do not provide logically self-sufficient values.[9]

The notion of a basic value, not subject to further analysis, is found in G.E. Moore's idea of goodness as a simple non-natural property;[10] this too was designed to terminate what would otherwise be a regress of justification in questions of value. But it remains to be settled whether we have the right to terminate the regress, or whether the Moorean notion is not open to the same objections as were pleasure and wealth. Plato thought he had a satisfactory answer to this demand. The transcendent and separate Form of Good represents an attempt to abstract value away from all other qualities, so that understanding its nature will ensure insight into all other values.[11]

Aristotle rejects this idea of Plato's; and his arguments against it are important in the development of his own positive account of value. He objects that 'good' is not a simple semantic unit; it does not bear the same meaning, and is not open to the same paraphrases in all of its occurrences.[12] Aristotle's point has been rediscovered in recent philosophy with the analysis of 'good' as a distinctive kind of adjective. To say that something is a 'good knife' or a 'good game' is not to say that it is *both* good *and* a knife or a game. It is, rather, to say that it is good as a game or as a knife. The meaning and truth of the attribution of goodness is essentially affected by the other semantic unit in the predication—'knife' or 'game'.[13]

The need for this analysis is particularly clear in the case of such a predication as 'a good thief'. Since we are inclined to agree that it is not good to be a good thief, we shall not allow that a good thief is good; so the meaning of 'good' in the complex predicate 'good thief' cannot be separated from that of 'thief'. Generalising from this example, we may say that to be a good F is not to be good and F, but rather good as F; and in that case it is a mistake to suppose with Plato or Moore that 'good' is a separate semantic unit or that goodness is a simple property.

Let us look at the reasoning which led Plato to discover supreme value in the simple and absolute Form of Good. However closely related are the two elements in the complex predicate 'good F', they are still distinct: to say that something is a good game or a good thief is not to say that it is a game game or a thief thief. Yet Plato agrees that 'good' does not have precisely the same meaning when it occurs in various combinations with other predicates. So he maintains that the central and essential meaning of the term is to be discovered not from these usages; instead, the word is to be inspected in contexts where it occurs uncombined with any other predicate. It is because of this semantic theory that he insists that value is best understood in abstraction from any particular context.[14]

Plato could appeal to our earlier sentence about the goodness of thieves. If it is not good to be a good thief, not only does this show the non-absolute character of the goodness of thieves; it seems also to show the absolute character of their lack of goodness. The second occurrence of 'good' in the sentence 'it is not good to be a good thief' is certainly not a predicate that stands independently of other elements in the sentence; but the case seems different with the first occurrence of 'good'. The surface grammar of the sentence indicates that it should be construed as stating that a good thief is simply not *good*, rather than not *a good such-and-such*. On the surface we have two uses of 'good', of which one is relative to other concepts but the other is absolute. Plato's thesis is that the absolute usage is the more fundamental; it illuminates the relative usage, not vice versa.

Aristotle objects that Plato has been badly misled by this surface grammar. He argues that all occurrences of 'good', even where it seems to be used absolutely, in fact presuppose its accompaniment by another predicate. At the same time he can explain the distinctive semantic role of the word in the complex predications of which it always, either explicitly or implicitly, forms a part.

Let us consider first contexts where 'good' explicitly qualifies another predicate. We need an account of the meaning of the word which should meet the following requirements. 'Good' is to mean something different from the various predicates with which it combines; preferably it is to have the same meaning, or at least connected meanings, in all these combinations. At the same time its meaning or meanings must be such that it needs the complementation of the other predicate. Aristotle maintains that these requirements are met by analysing goodness in terms of the fulfilment of function. To be a good such-and-such is to fulfil the function of that such-and-such.[15] This provides a constant thread of meaning running through the very different uses of 'good', and also makes it clear why the word is not a straightforwardly independent semantic unit.

This part of Aristotle's analysis is intended to accommodate Plato's claim that the concept of goodness cannot be reduced to the other concepts with which it is found to be joined. But he differs from Plato in not supposing that it is either desirable or possible to encounter goodness in actual isolation from any other concept. The first occurrence of 'good' in the sentence 'it is not good to be a good thief' is to be construed otherwise than as surface grammar suggests. Here Aristotle's essentialism enters the argument. Whatever is a thief, is so accidentally; this is an attribute that can be gained and lost without significant alteration of identity. But according to essentialism not all attributes are like this. In order to be identified at all, any object requires essential attributes; and so whatever is a thief accidentally will be something essentially. It is clear, moreover, what it must be essentially—a person.

We can now see what lies behind the judgement that a good thief is not good: he is not good because he is not *a good person*. Since personhood is an essential attribute of anything which happens also to be a thief, it is not necessary to spell out explicitly the accompanying concept.[16] 'Good' is used in a way that appears to be absolute. In reality it carries an implicit reference to the essential concept which is appropriate to the particular case. Aristotle can take it as support for his essentialism that the essential concept need only be implicit, thereby creating the illusion of an absolute notion of goodness.

There is a more informal way of making Aristotle's point which does not rely on the distinction between essential and accidental attributes. We do not judge a thing independently of all conceptual context; and if we attempt to do so, the wrong judgement is liable to be returned. A thief is a physical object, and also a living creature; he is also perhaps a doctor, a footballer, and a Greek. But it is not on the basis of any of these attributes that we condemn him; nor do we do so without reference to any attribute. We can exclude the last suggestion because it would not explain why the other concepts—physical object, Greek, etc.—play a thoroughly *subsidiary* role in our valuations.

Human persons are irreducibly different from other living creatures that may think and feel, such as gods and animals.[17] It follows that if there is no absolute concept of goodness that transcends all more specialised forms of it, the particular form that interests us will be the goodness of human persons. The nature of value, of the most fundamental kind that analysis can reveal, is to be discovered by examining human nature. To be good is to fulfil the function of a human person. Aristotle's strategy in ethics is explicitly one of deriving value from fact; and the complex argument which we have just examined is his defence of this strategy. Plato's search for a form of goodness which is not specific to humankind is bound to lead to a seriously distorted view of value.

Goodness and Human Nature

We must start with the main facts about human nature. Principal among these is the human ability to think and reason. But this rational power does not exhaust human nature; and while some of our reasoning is directed to abstract objects and has no tendency to issue in action, some is most certainly concerned with what we are to do.[18] For thought to produce action we need motivation. This is provided by the other main element in human nature—will and desire.[19] The intimate relation between thought and desire in the genesis of action, and the importance of both for an adequate idea of human nature, is well captured in Aristotle's characterisation of choice: 'Choice is either appetitive reason or intellectual appetite; an orginating source of this kind is the human.'[20]

These ideas, obvious though they seem, set the programme for the detailed treatment of virtue and vice which makes up Aristotle's work in ethics. The basic unit of value is the person; and what he is praised or blamed for are dispositions, habits which are exercised over a period of time. These dispositions, which fall into two kinds, are the virtues and vices: those of character are exhibited in the regulation of actions and emotions; those of intellect involve the exercise of every kind of thought. These two kinds of disposition can be distinguished in analysis, but in actual life they interact; a character is the product of actions and emotions regulated by thought, and a habit of thought is in the main directed upon action. The separation of the two by analysis is still a matter of great importance, first, because the kind of rationality which is morally valuable is exhibited in *action*, and secondly, because the primary bearer of moral properties is not the action itself but the settled character of the *agent*.

The argument so far is Aristotle's corrective to a Platonic account of goodness which removes it from the specific sphere of human action. He confronts this account with a detailed criticism of the way in which it construes 'good'; and he points out the more general objection that it ignores the active and appetitive aspects of human nature. The full significance of the Aristotelian conception of *virtue* can only be appreciated from his rich and thorough review of the many facets of human character, in each one of which we can function well or badly. Thus we learn that one should avoid not only cowardice and dishonesty, but also pusillanimity and shyness.[21] The full details occupy Books 2 to 5 of the *Nicomachean Ethics*. In Chapter 2 we got some flavour of the discussion and of the issues it can illuminate, when we examined the case of ambition.[22]

Virtue and Knowledge

There is still a threat to Aristotle's whole enterprise. The arsenals of the Socratic paradoxes are not yet exhausted; they contain some potent artillery which can be deployed in defence of Plato's championship of the supremacy of reason. Aristotle agrees with Plato that only rational action, performed from deliberate intent, is moral action;[23] but he accuses Plato of ignoring everything besides reason that is needed for moral action to occur. Suppose that Plato conceded that reason alone might not be enough to motivate action; he may still see no problem for an uncompromisingly intellectualist account of moral action. According to this account, what a person does is to be explained in terms of his beliefs about what it is best to do. Some of these beliefs are true; in principle, they can amount to knowledge. Aristotle is in agreement with Plato about objectivity and truth in moral judgement.[24] Once this is admitted, and the psychological significance of intellectual causes of action is agreed, it is hard to resist the conclusion that any non-intellectual motives occupy an essentially subsidiary position.

Plato worked out the argument for this position as he defended the Socratic identification of virtue and knowledge in the *Protagoras*. His strategy in this argument is to take any factor claimed by his opponent as a more efficacious spring of action than reason, and show that this can be construed as a reason for action as easily as anything else which the opponent will recognise as a reason: indeed, it quickly becomes hard to see how any of the opponent's factors could influence action in any way other than by being reasons for it. Plato uses pleasure as his example. This might well seem to be the kind of factor that could exert a greater influence on action than reason does, and in such a way that it counteracts the conclusion of reason. But Plato argues that if pleasure is to influence an agent, it must do so through his intellectual grasp of it. In other words, the reasonable agent must see pleasure as a reason for action if it is to exert any causal influence on his action.[25]

This strategy poses an unavoidable challenge to Aristotle's more cautious attitude to the role of reason in human action; and he confronts it in two separate passages. The first occurs in a general analysis of the limits of voluntary action (*E.N.* Γ1-5). Two kinds of ground are available for ruling that an action is not voluntary—when it is done under physical compulsion, or when it is done through ignorance. Aristotle follows common sense in allowing these factors as excuses, but he is stern in restricting their application. Force, for example, is not extended beyond the strictly physical; actions done under threat or internally generated emotional pressure represent kinds of duress that do not fall within this category of excuse.[26]

Similarly with ignorance; not every kind renders an action involuntary. Socrates would reason as follows: everyone wants to do what is good, the bad man does what is other than good, therefore insofar as the bad man does what he thinks he wants, he does not know what he does. Aristotle agrees with Socrates on the objectivity of the distinction between good and bad, and he does not dissent from any of the steps in this argument. But he sees that they need careful interpretation, since they are liable to lead to the conclusion that all wrong action is excusable because done from ignorance.[27]

Aristotle appeals to two main lines of argument to defuse the Socratic paradox, and their interpretation needs some care if they are not to seem lame. First, he notes that our habits of blaming, punishing and seeking to correct wrong action, all bear witness to our conviction that even if such actions involve ignorance, they cannot be excused by it.[28] This consideration might not impress the committed Socratic. We are familiar today with the view that punishment and allied practices are justified, if justified at all, otherwise than in terms of the fault of the persons on whom they are visited. Those who think this way will see no affront to common sense in the interpretation Aristotle gives to Socrates' view.

But Aristotle has more to say against the Socratic view. He notes that we punish people not merely for their actions but also for the state of mind in which those actions are performed.[29] Socrates suggests a certain kind of excuse which will remove blame from wrong action; common opinion rates this excuse as bringing its own special type of blame. If someone were to protest that the ignorance is constitutional to the agent, then it should be replied that this constitution is itself subject to blame and correction, since its presence and absence can be cultivated.[30] Of course, it could be maintained that all these attributions of blame are misguided. But Aristotle's point is that it is no answer to the common sense recognition that wrong action involves ignorance, to say that the ignorance must be such as to excuse the action; a much more radical subversion of ordinary habits of judgement is the only course that can consistently be pursued.

His second argument against this form of the Socratic paradox relies on an appeal to parity in our attitudes to good and bad action. If bad action is involuntary, so also must good action be; and conversely, if good action is voluntary, so also is bad action. A person who acts well has chosen so to act, and it must therefore have been possible for him to have chosen to act otherwise—to act badly. So there is nothing incoherent about the notion of making a bad choice; this notion is presupposed by that of a good choice.[31] Even if nobody actually chooses to do wrong, bad choice must be retained as a conceptual possibility if there is to be any choice at all.

We might object that the alternative to choosing a good action is not necessarily to choose a bad action: it might be choosing another good action, or choosing not to act at all. But these would be quibbles. We have started from a concern to emphasise the praiseworthy, because voluntary, character of correct choice. We praise it precisely because it succeeds in avoiding a wrong choice; and so Aristotle is right to insist that to question the possibility of choosing wrongly is to deprive oneself of the means for praising any choice as correct.[32]

This argument will not be effective against every target. The psychological determinist[33] will happily accept that all action is equally involuntary, and that the distinction between right and wrong action has nothing to do with voluntariness, if indeed this distinction can be sustained at all. But Socratic intellectualism, with its identification of virtue and knowledge, is not immune in this way. For to possess the knowledge which is necessary and sufficient for right action, is a praiseworthy thing;[34] and so the exercise of this knowledge in action must involve choice. Once this is granted, Aristotle's argument goes through.

The Socratic position is not offered primarily as an exercise in the philosophy of action; and this is why it should not be read as a form of psychological determinism. Socrates is concerned to commend a way of life, the quest for knowledge of goodness, and he bases his case on a particular view about the relation between thought and action. All reasons for action are commensurable, so that they produce a unique and computable result. Plato specifically considers how pleasure might be used to mount a challenge to this account; he argues that considerations of pleasure and pain must enter the calculation. Aristotle will not accept the analysis of action; his opposition chiefly turns on the morally unsatisfactory consequences of Plato's thesis. Plato misrepresents and undermines our right to praise the actions of the man of moral understanding.

Aristotle notes that it is tempting to say that 'nobody is willingly bad or unwillingly happy',[35] but only the second part of this claim can stand. There is a real limitation to the voluntariness of virtue. For it brings happiness, which everyone wants; and the virtuous person knows this. The mistake is in supposing that it follows that non-virtuous action is also involuntary. The vicious person does what he wants, even though he wants happiness and this is not delivered by what he does. Aristotle's dialectical device is to highlight the voluntariness of vice by contrasting it with the involuntariness of virtue. If no happy person wishes to be otherwise, can it really be a voluntary condition? But of course virtue is voluntary. One would only find it difficult to accept that vice is voluntary if one thought that the attractions of virtue were so clear as to exclude it from the province of objective knowledge. This is obviously wrong; the virtuous know what they are about.

This is Aristotle's diagnosis of the main error in Plato's intellectualist analysis of the mainspring of action. No analogous difficulty could arise with, for example, soundness and error in mathematical thought. Someone who asserts the primacy of emotive drive in action will also be incapable of recognising the subtle difference between the voluntariness of virtue and vice. The merit of Aristotle's analysis is that it reveals the need for a distinction. I maintain that this discriminatory attitude is available only to the philosopher who understands that the main issue is in moral philosophy rather than in the philosophy of action.

Weakness of Will

There is a whole further dimension to the problem bequeathed by the Socratic paradoxes. The cases which we have been considering so far, and which are discussed in *E.N.* Γ, are ones in which the agent does what he believes to be right. Aristotle agrees with Plato that this belief is mistaken, and his dispute is over the question of whether the mistake removes blame. But both would agree that what the agent does is straightforwardly consistent with what be believes (culpably or otherwise) to be right.

A different kind of case is discussed in *E.N.* H1-3, under the name of *akrasia*. This is conventionally rendered 'weakness of will' or 'incontinence', and although neither of these labels accurately marks the phenomenon, the conundrum to which they point is a classic in moral philosophy and the philosophy of action. 'Incontinence' suggests too strongly an involuntary physical process, while 'weakness of will' errs in the opposite direction. I shall use the latter label for reasons of convention and convenience.[36]

The kind of person Aristotle wishes to discuss is one who 'acts through an affection, knowing that what he does is bad'.[37] Common sense asserts that there are such people, and Aristotle is no more disposed here than elsewhere to disagree with common sense. But he recognises that this view creates a problem which gains cutting edge from Socrates' claims about the relation between knowledge and action. The problem can take two forms. Some philosophers acknowledge that there is a real difficulty in reconciling Socrates' argument with the insights of common sense; for others the only problem is to see why the first group find a problem here. Can a person act against his better knowledge? The first group find the difficulties raised by Socrates' argument so daunting that they deny that this person really has such knowledge. The opposite reaction is to see no difficulty whatever in this idea: many factors, of varying strength, cause actions, and there is no reason why the agent's knowledge of the right action should prevail among these many possible motives.[38]

Aristotle argues that this second position is self-evidently unacceptable. His conception of the distinctive nature of practical reasoning commits him to seeing it as essentially productive of action. In practical reasoning an action follows necessarily from certain premisses; and the necessity here is every bit as strong as in the case of theoretical reasoning, where what follows necessarily from the premisses is a statement.[39] This general view of practical reasoning would become untenable if we were prepared to admit cases in which the premisses were present but did not produce the action which they logically entailed. The force of the Socratic insight is that neither the agent nor we, as spectators to his action, could make sense of such an occurrence. Surely we must find some alternative description of these cases or risk destroying our facility for explaining any rational action.

So weakness of will, when described in terms of the agent's knowledge, does pose a problem; the temptation is to avoid it by denying that the weak-willed agent really knows the wrongness of his action. *If* he knew this, his action would be inexplicable; so we infer from his behaviour that, appearances notwithstanding, he lacks this knowledge. The proverb 'actions speak louder than words' embodies the same recognition of the importance of preserving a tight logical link between an agent's reasons and his actions. But merely to charge the weak-willed person with a hypocritical mouthing of statements which do not express his true reasons is no more satisfactory as an explanation of the phenomenon than is the dismissal of it as unproblematic. A real difficulty is not so much explained—or explained away—as ignored. Plato offered a subtler answer: the weak-willed person has belief, rather than knowledge, of what ought to be done.[40]

Recent debate about weakness of will has not taken much notice of the distinction between knowledge and belief. Yet the philosophical interest of Aristotle's discussion is due in considerable measure to the fact that it is his starting point. The substitution of 'believes' for 'knows' in the characterisation of the weak-willed person is attractive because belief can vary in a way not open to knowledge. Since what a person believes is not tied to truth, unlike what he knows, it is plausible to suppose that the weak-willed person continues to act on his beliefs when he acts wrongly, even though at other times his beliefs help him to see the wrongness of his actions. If he ever *knew* that such action was wrong, the connection between his conscious state at the moment of weak-willed action and his normal intentions would be too tenuous; this knowledge would be wholly missing in the weak-willed moment. There is no similar bar to the idea that his state might all along be one of belief and thus consistent in its characterisation. A person's beliefs can vary vastly over time and still be his beliefs; with knowledge, consistency is imposed by the constraint that it be true.

Plato's suggestion, then, is that we are strictly wrong to attribute knowledge to the weak-willed person when we say that he does what he *knows* to be wrong. His intentions at other times show that he never really knows this; and we only speak loosely when we give his state of mind the courtesy title of 'knowledge'. But Aristotle shows that this too is an inadequate response to the problem. He raises two difficulties. First, beliefs may be just as securely anchored in the agent's mind as knowledge is.

So if Plato finds it unintelligible that some particular item of knowledge should govern action to which it applies, he ought to find this equally unacceptable at least in the case of strongly held beliefs.[41] But if he replies that belief is intrinsically less well entrenched than knowledge, so that no belief can be as secure as knowledge, Aristotle brings a further objection. For, secondly, it must be remembered that weakness of will is a blameworthy disposition. We blame the agent for failing to act on his convictions; but for the charge to stick, the conviction must be of some tenacity. There may be nothing surprising, but equally there is nothing blameworthy, if someone fails to act on a belief which is weakly or tentatively held.[42] The more Plato emphasises the generally insecure nature of belief, the harder he makes it for himself to meet the requirements of morality on an adequate account of weakness of will.

Through these criticisms Aristotle shows how the topic of weakness of will involves issues both in psychology and in ethics. If the problem is conceived only in psychological terms, abandonment of each and every principle will exemplify it equally. But Aristotle dismisses as sophistry the suggestion that we need to consider the case where someone performs a good action by failing to stick to wicked principles. Is this, the sophist asks, a non-culpable case of weakness of will? Aristotle replies that, since obviously it is not culpable, we must realise that weakness of will involves failure to adhere not just to any principle, but to one that is correct and known to be such.[43]

Aristotle's aim, then, is to bring the problem of weakness of will into clearer focus, and to oppose those who attempt to recast in other terms the common sense view that it is possible to do what is wrong while knowing what is right. Weak-willed action is wrong, and the weak-willed person is disposed to wrong action. His fault is the distinctive one of failing to act on his knowledge of the correct thing to do.[44] This is what needs to be explained, and in a way that does not upset a general analysis of the basis of action in reason.

In his own account Aristotle uses analytical distinctions some of which had not been drawn by earlier investigators. He notes that to speak of what a person 'knows', or 'is aware of', is ambiguous, depending on whether we mean the possession of knowledge or its exercise and application.[45] The distinction is important in moral philosophy because we are interested in the way in which knowledge is exhibited in particular actions. A second refinement which he brings to the discussion concerns the different kinds of reason which occur as premisses of action. These are essentially two—general rules of the form 'actions of such-and-such a type should be done', and particular observations of the form 'these circumstances are such-and-such'; and although there may be some roughness in assigning some premisses to one or other of these categories, the general division between them is clear enough. It follows that a person may fail to produce the action which would be expected from his knowledge of some premiss, because knowledge of the other premiss needed for that action is missing. In that case he might know what ought to be done and yet, for lack of some further requisite knowledge, fail to act accordingly.[46]

But though these distinctions may instil a proper caution about dismissing as incoherent the statements by which common sense characterises weakness of will, they are insufficient by themselves to meet the challenge posed by the Socratic argument. Aristotle must show that the weak-willed action can be explained in terms of the agent's conscious intentions and that no further factor enters to nullify their causal role. Only in this way can he establish that the proper locus of blame is the relation between his motives and his action. He focuses on the factor, pleasure, which Plato had argued can cause action only by being included in the agent's rational intentions. Aristotle has to find a sense in which Plato's claim is true for the weak-willed action and a sense in which it is false.

Pleasure is a cause of action in two distinguishable ways: it may be a consciously entertained reason for doing something, or it may operate directly as a motive force on the agent's body.[47] We could dramatise the contrast by saying that in the first case the action is performed because it is thought to be pleasant, and in the second because it is pleasant. But it is necessary to avoid suggesting that pleasure might be an unconscious motive force or that the consciousness of it might fail to motivate. Still, Aristotle can appeal to the distinction to reveal the structure of weak-willed rationality. Suppose that someone is aware that an individual action, available for immediate performance, is of a kind that promotes pleasure. But he also knows that action of this kind is wrong. He will conclude that the action is pleasant; but in the absence of any general policy of pursuing pleasure, he will not perform the action, since it follows logically from his recognition of the wrongness of such actions that this particular one is not done. Yet he does it. The action is weak-willed because it is opposed to one which follows logically from his reasons for acting; but it is voluntary and intentional because the agent is fully aware of the factor which causes the action.[48]

Aristotle does not consider whether factors other than pleasure are able to play the double causal role which is needed for his analysis. Probably he selects this factor because it is the very one that Plato tried to remove as the basis for objection to his analysis of knowledge and action. Pleasure is an obvious example of something that is available to the agent's rational awareness and yet can cause action otherwise than by being a goal of rational policy. If other candidates can satisfy these requirements, they can be used in the same pattern of analysis. What is most important for Aristotle is that he should show that weak-willed action is caused by premisses which are included among the agent's reasons for action, while also making it clear that this particular action is not a reasonable one for this particular agent.[49]

The hallmark of weakness of will is that there should be reason for the unreasonableness of the action in which it is exhibited; and this must be reflected in a successful analysis of it. What has to be made sense of and explained, is something that the agent himself cannot fully understand; but the only resources available to function as premisses in the explanation are items from his own conscious state. If the weak-willed person concludes that his action is either readily intelligible or incomprehensible, his thought will echo the two philosophical reactions to the phenomenon which we noted at the start of this discussion. His moral progress away from the disposition to weakness of will depends on his recognising that there is a failure of match between what gives him reason to act, thereby causing his action, and what he accepts as a reasonable action. Analysis of what makes his action odd will show him how to bring what he does into closer connection with what he knows. So his action will show moral improvement as it comes to match the goodness which he understands.

Aristotle's discussion of weakness of will is a good illustration of two general features of his ethics: moral questions and the analysis of action are worked together, and so also are conceptual issues and positive prescriptions for conduct. To omit one or more of these dimensions from the conception of the problem is to fail to draw the full lesson from what Aristotle has to say about it.

Notes

1 See D. Davidson, 'How is Weakness of Will Possible?', repr. in *Essays on Actions and Events* (Oxford, 1980), p.30; D. Charles, *Aristotle's Philosophy of Action* (London, 1984), p.ix.
2 *E.N.* B2, 1103b26-30; K9, 1179a35-b4.
3 This is one of Aristotle's three works on ethics, the others being *Eudemian Ethics* and *Magna Moralia*. The *Eudemian Ethics* (which shares three books with *E.N.*) contains some interesting material; and from time to time it has been proposed that it rather than *E.N.* should form the basis of the study of Aristotle's ethics, most recently by A.J.P. Kenny, *The Aristotelian Ethics* (Oxford, 1978). But the consensus continues to give primacy to *E.N.*
4 *E.N.* B4, 1105a26-b9; cf. Γ2, 1111b5-6.
5 For Socrates' views, see T.H. Irwin, *Plato's Moral Theory* (Oxford, 1977), pp.6-7, 92-5.
6 Plato *Republic* 505-11.
7 Plato *Protagoras* 358c, 360d-1b; cf. *Meno* 78a6-b2.
8 See D.Z. Phillips, 'In Search of the Moral "Must": Mrs Foot's Fugitive Thought', *Philosophical Quarterly* 27 (1977), 140-57; J. McDowell, 'Are Moral Requirements Hypothetical Imperatives?', *Aristotelian Society Supplementary Volume* 52 (1978), 13-29.
9 *E.N.* A7, 1097a25-b8.
10 G.E. Moore, *Principia Ethica* (Cambridge, 1903), sections 5-15.
11 *Republic* 517c; 534b8-d1; cf. *Symposium* 210e2-11b5.
12 *E.N.* A6, 1096a23-9, 1096b21-6.
13 P.T. Geach, 'Good and Evil', and R.M. Hare, 'Geach: Good and Evil', both repr. in P. Foot (ed.), *Theories of Ethics* (Oxford, 1967), pp.64-73, 74-82; J.L. Mackie, *Ethics* (Penguin, 1977), pp.50-63.
14 Plato *Republic* 476a-b; cf. 524e-5a. The same idea occurs at *Sophist* 243e.
15 *E.N.* A7, 1097b24-33, 1098a8-11.
16 *E.N.* A7, 1097b33-8a5, 1098a16-18. For the importance of the idea that the goodness which matters in ethics is human goodness, cf. *E.N.* A13, 1102a13-15; Z5, 1140b20-1; Z7, 1141b6-14.
17 *Pol.* A3, 1253a27-9; cf. *E.N.* K7, 1177b26-8; H1, 1145a23-7.
18 *E.N.* Z1, 1139a3-15.
19 *E.N.* Z2, 1139a21-35; cf. *De An.* Γ10, 433a17-20.

[20] *E.N.* Z2, 1139b4-5.
[21] *E.N.* B7, 1107b21-3, 1108a31-4.
[22] Chapter 2, pp.36-9 above.
[23] *E.N.* B4, 1105a28-34; Γ1, 1111a22-4.
[24] *E.N.* Γ1, 1110b28-30; Z2, 1139a26-31.
[25] Plato *Protagoras* 353c-d, 355c-d.
[26] *E.N.* Γ1, 1110a1-13, 1111a27-b3.
[27] *E.N.* Γ1, 1110b28-1a6.
[28] *E.N.* Γ5, 1113b21-30; cf. the remarks on the educative power of law and punishment at *E.N.* K9, 1179b34-80a24.
[29] *E.N.* Γ5, 1113b30-4a3.
[30] *E.N.* Γ5, 1114a3-21; cf. B1, 1103a25-b25.
[31] *E.N.* Γ5, 1113b6-14.
[32] *E.N.* Γ5, 1114a31-b25.
[33] I always mean by 'determinism' what some distinguish as hard determinism, since the label seems to me to lose all dialectical value if it does not exclude the free and voluntary. The psychological determinist makes an appearance at *E.N.* Γ5, 1114a31-b1.
[34] Plato *Protagoras* 352c-d; cf. *E.N.* H2, 1145b23-4; H3, 1147b13-17.
[35] *E.N.* Γ5, 1113b14-15.
[36] The bibliography of this topic and Aristotle's discussion is extensive. The following give a good sense of the main issues in the original problem and its continuing afterlife: A.J.P. Kenny, 'The Practical Syllogism and Incontinence', *Phronesis* 11 (1966), 163-84; G. Santas, 'Aristotle on Practical Inference, the Explanation of Action and Akrasia', *Phronesis* 14 (1969), 162-89; Davidson, 'How is Weakness of Will Possible?', (see n.1 above); D. Wiggins, 'Weakness of Will, Commensurability, and the Objects of Deliberation and Desire', *Proceedings of the Aristotelian Society* 79 (1978–79), 251-77.
[37] *E.N.* H1, 1145b12-13.
[38] See E.J. Lemmon, 'Moral Dilemmas', *Philosophical Review* 71 (1962), pp.143-8. This view is also suggested by R.R.K. Sorabji, *Necessity, Cause and Blame* (London, 1980), p.31.
[39] *M.A.* 7, 701a9-25; *E.N.* H3, 1147a24-8; see G.E.M. Anscombe, 'Thought and Action in Aristotle', in R. Bambrough (ed.), *New Essays on Plato and Aristotle* (London, 1965), pp.143-58.
[40] *E.N.* H2, 1145b31-5.
[41] *E.N.* H3, 1146b24-31.
[42] *E.N.* H2, 1145b36-6a4.
[43] *E.N.* H2, 1146a27-31.
[44] *E.N.* H2, 1146b19-22; H8, 1150b29-31.
[45] *E.N.* H3, 1146b31-5; cf. *De An.* B5, 417a24-30. This distinction is anticipated in Plato *Theaetetus* 197b-c.
[46] *E.N.* H3, 1147a1-10; cf. *E.N.* Z7, 1141b14-22.
[47] Cf. the distinction between kinds of pleasure at *E.N.* Γ10, 1117b28-18a6; the notion of pleasure as physically motivating is well captured at *E.N.* H13, 1153b25-35.
[48] *E.N.* H3, 1147a31-b3.

[49] This is the force of the apparent concession to Socrates at *E.N.* H3, 1147b13-17. Aristotle does not agree with Socrates that the weak-willed agent lacks knowledge of what he does.

CHAPTER 9

Politics

Aristotle's ethical theory is different from some more recent theory; it does not take altruism as one of its basic premisses.[1] There is no special emphasis on the importance of other people. He simply recommends each person to pursue his own happiness. The individual's happiness is not secured at the expense of others, but neither does it appear significantly to depend on that of others; and with his remarks about the importance of self-sufficiency Aristotle warns against any theory which would make such dependence excessive.[2]

The altruistic aspects of individual action are not ignored. They are most prominent in the two books on friendship and the one on justice in the *Nicomachean Ethics*. Many of the dispositions analysed in his detailed discussion of the theory of the mean could not be coherently imagined outside a social context. The reason why Aristotle does not need to dwell on this point is that he regards ethics as continuous with politics. His work on politics—or more precisely, on the social dimension of human affairs—leads straight on from his discussion of ethics; and he makes it clear that politics is the logically prior study.[3] Human persons must belong to the kind of social organisation which a state is; any biological human of whom this is not true, is either a beast or a god.[4]

Politics is the study of the ways in which the pursuit of the good life can be affected by social structure, particularly by exercising rationality through decision-making. Ethics abstracts the individual from this larger context in which he must pursue the good life. This way of understanding the relation between the two studies is prefigured in earlier thinkers, especially Plato.

Aristotle finds major inadequacies in their work; and the steps which he takes to correct them provide one of the main reasons for the continuing importance of his own theory.

Slavery, the Family and the State

The totalitarian character of Plato's political theorising has been the subject of much adverse comment in recent scholarship.[5] His blueprint for the best state certainly contains features which support such criticism—censorship and central control of education, subordination of family relationships to the direction of the state, and above all the unchallenged power exercised by a permanent elite of experts.[6] Some of Plato's contemporaries who, like him, derived their inspiration from Socrates, advanced an uncompromising individualism in explicit opposition to Plato's advocacy of the civic regimentation of personal life.[7]

This criticism misses to some extent the rationale of Plato's political theory. His leading claim is not that either the state or the individual takes precedence over the other, but rather that both of them should be seen as on a par. Starting from the observation that the same language of value is applied to the individual and to the social unit,[8] Plato analyses the nature of excellence and of deviations from the ideal, as they appear in political organisations and also in the individual's life. The detailed investigation appears to confirm that it is sound strategy to mount parallel analyses of individual and social value. We are given an account of the nature of the individual person which shows that he is a combination of distinct psychological faculties, and an account of the state which attributes to it the same kind of organic unity to be found in the individual.[9] It is small surprise that Plato should subordinate the individual to the state of which he is a part, given the exact parallel between the structure of the two.

In opposing an individualism which fails to recognise the primary role played by the state in securing the good life, Aristotle is with Plato. But he finds deep flaws in the parallels that Plato draws between individual and state. He is particularly critical of the view of society as an organic unit; to regard society as a super-individual is to mistake both the complexity and the true nature of the various groupings which are necessary for our well-being. People come together in different kinds of association—the family, the household, the village, and the state;[10] and a leading requirement of satisfactory political theory is to understand the relations between these social groupings. It is significant that Aristotle's major criticism of Plato arises over his treatment of family ties and possessions. A necessary preliminary to the study of the state is to analyse the family and the other associations, not because they mirror the structure of the state but so that we can be alert to what distinguishes the state from them.[11]

Aristotle's account of these smaller groupings is directed at demonstrating how they benefit the natural aims of the participating individuals; and he is particularly interested in the relations of power among the participants. In these discussions he evinces attitudes about the naturalness of the institution of slavery, as well as of the superiority of men over women and Greeks over foreigners, that are rebarbative to modern sensibility. These attitudes which have often brought Greek political thought into disrepute do not in fact occupy a central position in Aristotle's theory; but their power to repel demands exorcism.

Aristotle takes some pains to defend his views on slavery. He maintains that the natural constitution of humans and animals supplies extensive indications of a division of functions into those of controller and controlled. This creates a *prima facie* basis for the idea that some persons are natural subordinates—slaves—to others who are natural directors—their masters. The objection to this division of persons is that in practice it can only operate in a way that is arbitrary and artificial.[12] The legal title of slave or master does not provide moral justification for the control by force of one person by another. Aristotle replies that while the objection is based on a fair point, it draws the wrong conclusion. Our sense of outrage at what the artificial processes of law can bring about in some cases of enslavement is directed at these particular abuses of morality, not at the morality of slavery itself; otherwise there would be no special problem about the examples of slavery which the objection relies on.[13]

We need to place the analysis of the relation between master and slave in the more general setting of Aristotle's political argument. A state is an association of free and equal persons;[14] but here too there arise issues of who is to control whom, and on what terms. Aristotle argues that the division of function between controller and controlled is as natural in the state as in the other social groupings. But in the state the question of who exercises either of these functions does not depend on nature; and this distinguishes the political grouping from the other associations.[15] The relation between master and slave has political significance only insofar as it points to the naturalness of a parallel but distinct social relation. Beyond that, the differences between master and slave, man and woman, or Greek and foreigner, do not enter in.[16]

The basis of Aristotle's criticism of Plato's ideal state is his recognition of the difference between the state and other groupings. His most insistent line of attack is directed against Plato's proposal to strengthen the unity of the state by making it a single family. The proposal will not work because it undermines the structure of any actual family within such a state; and so we would lose a potent force for the looser kind of cohesion which the state possesses. As Aristotle recognises, there is both a psychological and a logical difficulty in Plato's idea. The logical difficulty is this: for the sense of common kinship and possession to be realised, it is necessary that everyone should regard everybody else as belonging to them, as their own. But there is an ambiguity in this description. Either the desired result is achieved if and only if for each person there is someone else who regards him as his own; or every person is regarded by every other person as his own. The scope of 'his own' is wider on the first interpretation than on the second. But the second, narrow-scope interpretation is surely what Plato is trying to commend to us. The formula he actually uses does not compel us to understand his recommendation in this way.[17]

To insist on a narrow-scope interpretation is to invite the psychological objection. There are many clear differences in the ways in which we feel and act towards members of our family and the citizenry at large. There are, for example, taboos on sex within the family which are not normally regarded as applying in a larger context; and violent acts like parricide or matricide attract a special degree of opprobrium because of the family relationship.[18] Aristotle's objection to a radical proposal to extend the concept of the family does not rest merely on a conservative attachment to prevailing practices. His point cuts deeper. The proposal to extend the family is coherent only if we start with a particular idea of what a family is and what forms of behaviour are entailed by membership of it. Part of this idea involves distinguishing between members of the family and outsiders.[19] So one way to prevent the idea from being applied is to obliterate this distinction; and this is the burden of Aristotle's argument against Plato.

The Analysis of Constitutions

In his work on politics Plato uses the blueprint of an ideal state to measure the deficiencies of existing political systems. His aim is unequivocally normative, but incidentally he initiates the comparative physiology of politics. We are also introduced to its pathology, since he highlights the weaknesses of existing constitutions by analysing their propensity to break down in revolution. Aristotle carries the investigation of constitutions much further forward. So thorough and detailed is his commentary that he has been regarded as the champion of the empirical approach to the study of politics; he has been contrasted with Plato whose approach is characterised as normative.[20]

But this would be to oversimplify. Aristotle certainly uses a great deal of material from his investigations of actual constitutions, of which many were to be found in the fragmented political mosaic of the Mediterranean world. But all this empirical detail is pressed into the service of a normative end; Aristotle holds firm to the practical aim of helping his audience to live the best life.[21] Attention to the fine details of constitutional practice follows from this aim when properly executed. In politics as with other practical skills one needs to consider the intended beneficiaries of one's prescriptions. These will include some superlative specimens among the larger number of people who are aiming at excellence, so that some will be able to achieve a form of excellence that may not be available to the majority. There will be other people in the audience who do not have excellence in their sights; their aim is to preserve some lesser good related to their own circumstances. Every part of the broad audience must be allowed for, and every part can be. The methodological condition for success in this objective is to possess a sufficiently flexible interpretation of what it means to enhance the excellence of political life.[22]

This is a further example of the theory which underpins Aristotle's dialectical style of philosophy. Political analysis is a rational undertaking. Its goal is truth, and as a consequence some accounts will be superior to others simply by virtue of their correctness. But what constitutes correctness, and therefore truth, will be in part a matter of the nature of the audience being addressed. Aristotle is not a relativist. The composition of the audience does not by itself determine how satisfactory is the account which is being put to it. Dialectic helps us in each context of discussion to settle whether, and to what extent, the objective and subjective elements in the solution of a problem should predominate.[23]

So while there is much analysis and many recommendations in Aristotle's review of the main kinds of constitution, there is also an ineliminable imprecision. Aristotle distinguishes six main kinds of constitution: there is a threefold division according to the proportion of the members of the state who are in control, and this number is doubled because the three forms of control can be exercised well or badly. Where there is only one ruler, the constitution is either kingship or tyranny; a small number of rulers defines an aristocracy or oligarchy, and we have a republic or a democracy where everyone is in control. The good forms of constitution are kingship, aristocracy, republic; and the bad are tyranny, oligarchy, democracy.[24]

What in general distinguishes the bad from the good is the pursuit of sectional as opposed to universal benefit.[25] But while Aristotle maintains that this overall distinction among constitutions is the most fundamental—and one which was most damagingly missed by earlier political theorists[26]—it is far from straightforward. The reason is that democracy and the other deviant forms of constitution, even though flawed, are still genuine modes of political association; and they must therefore embody a greater degree of cohesion than would be produced merely by the physical juxtaposition and mercantile intermingling of a number of individuals.[27] The cohesion comes from a shared standard of justice. Justice is the regulation of goods in accordance with the equalities and inequalities that exist between the individuals who participate in a transaction. Different forms of justice will arise because democrats emphasise the equality of all citizens, while oligarchs emphasise their inequality; the just distribution of goods will vary according to these different valuations of persons.

So the bad forms of constitution have their political institutions; and Aristotle surveys in great detail their elements, and examines actual examples of them which he found in contemporary practice. But he constantly urges us not to confuse them with the good forms where the common interest of all citizens is pursued, however concentrated or diffuse the system of power. The theme of the naturalness of the state reappears here. It is an association which provides a good life for all its participants—and 'participants' means, in the specific context of the political relationship, those who are full citizens of the state.[28] Aristotle recognises some fluidity in the definition of a citizen. It is a serial notion, like that of the state, or the soul; and in Chapter 7 it was argued that no illuminating general account of the members of a series is possible.[29]

The character of a state depends on that of its citizens. To neglect the political importance of the individual is a certain prescription for totalitarianism; it also produces the inadequate classifications of constitutions which Aristotle wishes to correct. The logical relation between state and citizen also works in the reverse order. It is the particular constitution which defines who is a citizen and who is not.[30] When Aristotle discusses this question he often refers to features of the contemporary social situation—slaves, resident aliens, tradesmen. Not every human being who inhabits a particular geographical area should be automatically regarded as participating in the political process. Everyone can see the force of this exclusion in the case of children or the insane. So Aristotle's principle is clear; somewhere a line must be drawn between citizen and non-citizen. The distinction between constitutions provides the best logical support for the idea that someone who is a citizen under one constitution, may well not be under some other. Democracies and republics are likely to be more accommodating in the extension of citizenship than constitutions where power is concentrated in fewer hands.[31]

If being a rational adult person is not a sufficient condition for citizenship, some further criterion must be found which will determine who is and who is not a citizen. Perhaps the requisite criterion is the possession (if only through the rarely used sanction of the quinquennial ballot-box vote) of ultimate political power. So constitutions where the majority exercise rule—democracies and republics—can easily seem preferable to more restrictive constitutions. But Aristotle does not place such high value on majority rule. Democracy is a deviant constitution; and republic, the non-deviant form of majority rule, is the least ideal of the good political systems. We must now consider why Aristotle takes this view.

If the character of the state follows from that of its citizens, its excellence will depend on theirs. What is it to be a good citizen? The intimate connection in Aristotle's thought between ethics and politics suggests that the answer will come from ethics: to be a good citizen is to be a good person. But on reflection this is not plausible. People come in varying degrees of goodness, and it is characteristic of a state to consist of dissimilar people. Moreover the goodness of the citizen will consist both in the giving of commands and decisions and in complying with those of other citizens. It is possible, therefore, to have a good state consisting of citizens all of whom possess equally the goodness of citizens but whose goodness as individuals varies in degree.[32]

The constitution which best reflects these complex conditions of excellence is one where power is restricted to the few rather than shared by the many. Aristotle's preferred constitution is aristocracy or even, if it can be achieved in practice, kingship.[33] Less admirable, but still a fundamentally good form of constitution, is a republic. Here political power is widely diffused; but since this constitution combines the best features of both oligarchy and democracy, there is scope to give recognition to the superior virtue of some of the citizens.[34]

Aristotle's proposals for the exercise of constitutional power are thoroughly elitist, but it is important to appreciate how his elitism differs from that of Plato. He considers, and rejects, the argument behind Plato's proposal to reserve power to a minority. This argument is based on the superior political expertise of the inevitably small number of people who can achieve the highest level of education. Their right to political power parallels the doctor's right to power in medical matters. Aristotle finds this argument unconvincing. Those who are ruled are consumers of the ruler's prescriptions, and like the audience at a play they have an expertise to set alongside that of the ruler. It is not knowledge but virtue that is the basis of rule; and since we are considering good constitutions, the virtue of the other citizens will serve to ensure that the superior virtue of the ruler is recognised.[35]

The review of the six main kinds of constitution, and of the different manifestations of each of these kinds, is immensely detailed and supported by very many references to actual historical states. Here Aristotle uses the researches which he organised into the history of 157 states in the Mediterranean world. It is this aspect of the discussion in the *Politics* which has led commentators to label his approach empirical. Some have even argued that the work is an ill coordinated amalgam of empirical and theoretical elements.

Both these judgements are mistaken. At the centre of Aristotle's conception of political structure and activity is the view that human rationality is the dominant factor. What defines a political system is the idea of justice which directs the decisions of those who participate in the state.[36] Such an idea is not formed in a vacuum but is fed by experience of the ways in which institutions and policies lead to particular results, whether desirable or undesirable. So the citizens of a state are bound to consider the lessons of actual political practice as they reflect on the just ideal.

In politics, as in ethics, Aristotle's aim is the practical one of enabling his audience to achieve the best life. So he must look to the experience afforded by historical states; the insights yielded by such an examination will enhance his own understanding and will also assist the audience to reach a satisfactory idea of justice. Thus the empirical material is put unequivocally at the service of a normative and theoretical interest. Aristotle's final conclusion is that when his audience has understood the true nature of justice, they will see that superior virtue merits the reservation of political power to a limited number of citizens. To recognise a non-democratic constitution as the best kind of state is a political achievement of a population with the virtue of citizenry.[37]

Revolution

The intimate connection between theory and practice in politics is very clear in Aristotle's analysis of revolution. Greek intellectuals had been interested in revolution ever since Thucydides provided his remarkable cameo of the violent revolutions which were provoked by the early years of the Peloponnesian War nearly a century before Aristotle wrote on politics.[38] Thucydides speaks not only of the physical violence but also of the intellectual upheaval which formed this revolutionary pattern. Words and concepts were as unstable as ownership of property or titles of contract. The most striking feature of the picture is the impermanence, indeed the incommensurability of moral values in a period of revolutionary change.

The disruption of moral theory provides the leading idea in Aristotle's discussion of revolution. In a revolution one constitution normally gives place to another; at the very least, there is a radical replacement of the ruling group within a single form of constitution. What defines each constitution is the conception of justice it embodies; and it is a change in this conception which above all is responsible for revolution.[39] As changes occur in the criteria of equality and fairness on which citizens base their judgements of value, so the manner and extent of political power will alter. Those who are judged, and judge themselves, ineligible to rule because of their inequality with a group superior to them in some way, may come to focus their attention on some other respect in which they are equal to the group with superior power. As a consequence they will want to alter the constitutional basis which distributes power in what they now perceive to be an unfair and unequal way.[40] This is revolution. It is radical change; but as we saw in Chapter 5, even radical change needs an element of continuity,[41] and in revolution this is supplied by the participants' perceptions of what is just.

Throughout Book E of the *Politics*, which is given over to the analysis of revolution, Aristotle makes reference to actual examples of the phenomenon as he illustrates every kind of radical shift between constitutions, as well as within some of them. He frequently mentions causal factors external to the sense of justice of those engaged in the revolution. The proximity of differently constituted states and, in some cases, their aggression provide examples of such causal factors; and the increase in size of one economic class relative to another is an example of a causal factor internal to the state. These factors have figured very importantly in some analyses of revolution. They dominate the work of Machiavelli, Hobbes and Marx whose political theories are particularly notable for their attention to revolution. But in this subject the forerunner for these philosophers was Aristotle. So let us look in greater detail at what Aristotle says about how such external factors have a causal role in revolutions.

In one section of his analysis of the causes of revolution in aristocracies he refers to six actual cases of revolution.[42] Some of them occurred during war or during a process of colonisation; and he cites such stresses as having contributed to the revolution. But he also makes it clear that factors of this kind achieve their effect because of their impact on the revolutionaries' thought. They are moved to act by their interpretation of what is justly due to them in accordance with their own superior worth. They apply an aristocractic conception of justice to their own circumstances and find that the distribution of goods does not accord with their own merit. The purpose of the revolution is to correct this injustice, and as a result they actually alter the conception of justice which was the basis for their action. The leading theme in Aristotle's analysis is to assign the dominant causal role in these revolutions to the moral insights of those involved, not to the external factors which other philosophers rate so important.[43]

A further example of Aristotle's approach occurs in his analysis of revolution in democracies.[44] He produces five examples of how demagogues' indulgence of the mass of people can so alienate the wealthy as to provoke them to revolution. Here too there are certain kinds of external factor, involving matters of foreign or military policy, which play a part in bringing about the insurrectionary actions. But what is an essential factor in producing the revolution is the sense of injustice on the part of the wealthy whose assets are reduced by the demagogues.

A new political grouping is formed because of a shared perception. In a normal democracy the wealthy are not a significant constitutional factor; they become one by virtue of a united awareness of some injustice.[45] We see once again the primary role played by thought in promoting revolution.

Aristotle is concerned not only to analyse the causes of revolution but also to give advice on how to avoid it. Here too he concentrates mainly on the thoughts and evaluations of the people involved in the political process. He speaks of the cohesive effect which fear of an external enemy can have on a state. To preserve the constitution it may be necessary to avoid actions which would reinforce the population's sense of security. But the most important source of stability for a state is the education of its citizens.[46] Their education needs to be appropriate to the particular constitution of that state. Self-indulgence is destructive of oligarchy, and indiscipline of democracy; yet these are the very habits which the protagonists in each kind of constitution are liable to acquire. Only through education will people see that the avoidance of such habits preserves rather than destroys their self-interest.

A constitution is an embodiment of human thoughts and values. It contains laws and other institutional safeguards, but these will be inadequate unless the intellectual outlook of the citizens remains stable. A fully reflective awareness of the different forms of justice in different constitutions is needed just as much for the preservation as for the destruction of a state.

Political Theory and Practice

Aristotle's work on politics is firmly located in the context of his time. He wrote about the city-state, and his whole political theory is permeated by the assumption that a state of this modest size is the most developed unit of human association.[47] That assumption was grounded on Greek political experience during the two centuries preceding the composition of the *Politics*; but Alexander's conquests were about to wreak a fundamental change, with the city-state giving way to much larger political units.

Aristotle's political philosophy has not dated, largely because of its intellectual setting, which is the other aspect of its context.

In Plato's political theory he found a sustained attempt to base the right to political power on the possession of superior knowledge and rationality. Plato was motivated by opposition to relativism. He rejected the view that in politics the truth varies from society to society. The relativist approach to politics gained support as philosophers—especially the historians and the Sophists of the fifth century—came to appreciate the considerable variety of political constitutions in existence. Each functioned by its own standards. Who could say that any of these standards was wrong?

Plato was convinced that some, at least, were wrong; and he sought to undermine the relativist epistemology which produced a contrary conclusion. He argued for an objective, non-relative conception of political value. He took it to be a condition for the success of this conception, that the arrangements for political power in any particular state should play no part in determining the nature of political right. The experts' paradigm provides the means for adjudicating among the cultural relativities, not vice versa.[48]

Aristotle's reaction to this conflict is exactly the same as in his theory of ethics. He respects Plato's assertion of the sovereignty of reason; but he rejects his lack of concern with the rich and complex data of experience. Politics and ethics comprehend matters which are essentially more diffuse than the concerns of mathematics and the theoretical sciences; the role played by human persons guarantees that no simple paradigm will meet the case. So Aristotle takes great care to examine actual political phenomena. He shares with the Sophists a recognition that the diversity of details which such an examination reveals, cannot be ignored by a proper examination of political value. The empirical aspects of his work are no mere embellishment; they constitute the proper subject matter of the investigation of human political life.[49]

But the relativist's inference from this methodological requirement is wrong, and Plato's is right. Politics is a normative study. It does have as its aim the account of the best political organisation; and Aristotle's account, which is full of positive value-judgements, meets this requirement. To achieve the best social life we must reason about justice. The reasoning is more complex than Plato allowed; this much is clear from our analysis of Aristotle's comments on the different forms of constitution and on how they can be destroyed and preserved. There is no simple prescription which will tell anyone, anywhere, how he ought to participate in his social surroundings. However, this at least can be said: he ought to exercise his own political judgements. Aristotle aims to provide maximum assistance to enable him to do so. Plato prescribed that power should be held by philosophers. Aristotle does not disagree, but he tries to ensure that as many as possible will be able to philosophise.

Notes

1. Contrast B.A.O. Williams, 'Egoism and Altruism', repr. in *Problems of the Self* (Cambridge, 1973), pp.250-1.
2. *E.N.* K7, 1177a27-b1. The importance of friends is emphasised at *E.N.* A7, 1097b8-13, as it is at I9, 1169b16-22; but the fact that Aristotle needs to devote the latter chapter to debating the issue is revealing. For a discussion of the problem, see J.M. Cooper, 'Aristotle on Friendship', in A.O. Rorty (ed.), *Essays on Aristotle's Ethics* (California, 1980), pp.301-40.
3. *E.N.* A2, 1094a27-b11; *Pol.* Γ12, 1282b14-21.
4. *Pol.* A3, 1253a1-9, 25-9.
5. The classic statements are in R.H.S. Crossman, *Plato Today* (London, 1937), and K.R. Popper, *The Open Society and its Enemies*, vol.1 (London, 1945).
6. Plato *Republic* 414b-15c; 462-4.
7. E. Barker, *Greek Political Theory* (London, 1960), pp.120-4.
8. *Republic* 368e2-9a3.
9. *Republic* 441c-d.
10. *Pol.* A2, 1252b12-31.
11. *Pol.* A7, 1255b16-20; cf. *E.N.* E6, 1134b8-18.
12. *Pol.* A6, 1255a3-11, 24-8.
13. *Pol.* A6, 1255a29-32.
14. *Pol.* Γ13, 1283b27-4a3. The emphasis on equality here needs to be set beside Aristotle's observations on the importance, in preserving and subverting political systems, on *perceived* equalities and inequalities (cf. *Pol.* E1, 1301a25-b4). See W. von Leyden, *Aristotle on Equality and Justice* (Macmillan, 1985), pp.57-64.
15. *Pol.* A2, 1252a30-2; H14, 1332b12-41; cf. B2, 1261a37-b5.
16. This is not to endorse Aristotle's view of the naturalness of slavery, on which the modern reader will agree with M.I. Finley, *Ancient Slavery and Modern Ideology* (London, 1980), p.119. It is to emphasise that Aristotle's interest is not in defending slavery as such but in appealing to a widely held contemporary view of the institution to make a point about what does concern him, the political unit.

17 *Pol*. B3, 1261b16-32; cf. *S.E.* 30, 181b19-21.
18 *Pol*. B4, 1262a25-40.
19 *Pol*. B2, 1261b6-15.
20 See W. Jaeger, *Aristotle*, transl. R. Robinson (Oxford, 1948), pp.290-2. For a more accurate assessment, see R.G. Mulgan, *Aristotle's Political Theory* (Oxford, 1977), pp.7-12.
21 The practical benefits of the study of the best form of constitution are pointed out at *Pol*. B1, 1260b27-33; H1, 1323a14-19.
22 This methodology is set out in the notable chapter *Pol*. Δ1.
23 *Top*. Z4, 142a6-13; for the application to politics, cf. *Pol*. Δ2, 1289b17-19. See my 'Aristotle on Relativism', *Philosophical Quarterly* 24 (1974), 193-203.
24 *Pol*. Γ7; Δ2, 1289a26-30.
25 *Pol*. Γ7, 1279a28-31.
26 *Pol*. Γ9, 1280a7-b12; cf. Δ2, 1289b5-11; Δ7, 1293a35-b1.
27 *Pol*. Γ9, 1280b24-35.
28 *Pol*. Γ1, 1275a2-5, 22-9.
29 *Pol*. Γ1, 1275a33-b7; Chapter 7, pp.123-7 above.
30 *Pol*. Γ7, 1278a15-17; Γ13, 1283b42-4a1.
31 *Pol*. Γ1, 1275b5-7; cf. Γ5.
32 This question is thoroughly and subtly examined in *Pol*. Γ4; it is Aristotle's commentary on the strict parallel between individual and social value which underpins Plato's *Republic*.
33 *Pol*. Δ2, 1289a30-3; Δ7, 1293b1-7, 18-20; Γ13, 1284b25-34.
34 *Pol*. Δ8, 1293b33-4a9; Δ12, 1296b38-7a13.
35 *Pol*. Γ11, 1282a14-23. On this point, see R.G. Mulgan, *Aristotle's Political Theory* (Oxford, 1977), pp.104-6.
36 *Pol*. Γ9, 1280a7-25; 1281a8-10; Γ12, 1282b14-23.
37 *Pol*. Γ4, 1277b7-32; Γ9, 1281a4-8; Γ12, 1283a10-17.
38 Thucydides III 82-3; cf. C.W. Macleod, 'Thucydides on Faction (3.82-83)', *Proceedings of the Cambridge Philological Society* NS 25 (1979), 52-68.
39 *Pol*. E1, 1301a25-35, 1301b6-17.
40 *Pol*. E1, 1301a35-9; E2, 1302a24-31.
41 Chapter 5, pp.84-9 above.
42 *Pol*. E7, 1306b27-7a5.
43 A further example of Aristotle's approach is provided by his lengthy analysis of the causes of revolution in single-rule constitutions (kingship and tyranny) in *Pol*. E10 (see e.g. 1311a23-36).
44 *Pol*. E5, 1304b20-5a7.
45 *Pol*. Δ4, 1291b30-7; E5, 1305a3-7.
46 *Pol*. E9, 1310a12-36.
47 *Pol*. H4; cf. Γ3, 1276a24-30.
48 Plato *Republic* 592a-b.
49 *Pol*. Δ1, 1289a10-25.

CHAPTER 10

God

God, together with truth, goodness and reality, provides the subject matter of philosophy in the popular imagination. But while most philosophers today have something to say about the other three topics, on the question of God there appears to be almost total silence. To be sure, philosophy of religion flourishes, but only as a small subsection of philosophical study, hardly more prominent than philosophy of literature or music or sport. The layman who wants to learn more about God from the philosopher, usually has to be satisfied with answers such as Napoleon got from Laplace: 'I have no need of that hypothesis.'

When philosophy abandons the topic of God, even as a hypothesis, this creates a sense of lacuna. The history of philosophy is replete with substantial contributions to the topic. Aristotle was well aware of sceptical voices which would move him to have 'no need of the hypothesis'. But while he is conscious of the need for rigorous argument in this as in other areas of philosophy, the general principles of his philosophical method commit him to recognising the significance of a belief which is nearly universal. Atheism and agnosticism are not viable options for Aristotle; but a fideistic dismissal of the philosophers' doubts about commonsense religious belief is not acceptable either.[1]

Aristotle and the Philosophy of Religion

Aristotle is to be grouped neither with those philosophers who ignore theological issues nor with those who give them a central place in their thought. Berkeley and Descartes are examples of philosophers who gave God a central role in metaphysics. Berkeley made the existence of the world of our familiar experience depend on the mind of God, while Descartes used our certainty about God's existence to confer certainty on otherwise more obscure matters.[2]

Aristotle does not seek to reduce all investigation to theology. He characterises the position of theology among the other sciences as 'universal inasmuch as primary';[3] and while the full significance of this remark will become clear only after we have followed Aristotle's theological argument in detail, it is plainly his intention not to allow to the study of God the sort of unrestricted universality promised by the programme of a Berkeley. In Aristotle's view the study of things other than God can largely be pursued without reference to theology.

So theology occupies an important but not fundamental position in his scheme of studies. His account of the nature and causal role of God is derived from a combination of technical, philosophical analyses and reflections based on more popular ideas about what deserves worship. It is thoroughly characteristic of his philosophical method that he should examine a topic by converging from these two directions. The prevailing views from which discussion is to start, must include the positions adopted by the experts and also the deliverances of popular common sense.[4] This method holds generally for all investigation; with theology it produces a particularly striking result.

The problem of reconciling the God of the philosophers with the God of popular religion is a preoccupation of much theology. Even where it is allowed that the philosophers are saying something cogent, is it clear that what they are talking about is *God*? Conversely the claims of popular religion, while undoubtedly intended to be about God, for lack of argumentative cogency may fail to be about anything at all.[5] Aristotle's method is designed to meet these difficulties by requiring both approaches to theology to converge on a common solution.

His chief contribution to this subject comes in a large and intricate argument in *Metaphysics* Λ. He also discusses it in other works, notably in the *De Caelo*, *Physics* Θ, and the fragmentary *De Philosphia*; and it used to be thought that there were inconsistencies between the views expressed in these works, indicating that Aristotle's theories altered and developed. Often the direction of development was supposed to be away from an initial position close to Plato's, towards a rejection of the primacy of self-sustaining change.[6]

The claims to detect inconsistencies were premature. A better understanding of Aristotle's arguments in theology shows that his various statements are compatible; indeed they are all needed for a complete grasp of his theory. I shall concentrate on the ambitious argument of *Metaphysics* Λ and, at the same time, note the points at which his argument makes contact with his discussions in other works.

The First Cause of Change

His starting point is the phenomenon of change and the ensuing argument is cosmological in style. All change presupposes the existence of a first cause which does not itself undergo change. Aristotle's argument has two stages: the first establishes that all change has a single original cause, and the second that this object does not itself change. The first stage follows, though it also refines, a line of thought which was familiar to Aristotle's predecessors, especially Plato.[7] In the second stage Aristotle breaks new ground; and this is where he sees the principal achievement of his argument. The second stage is the one which carries most theological significance. It is consistent with Aristotle's methodology that he should attach special importance to the proof of the unchanging character of the first cause.

The argument opens by noting that it is incoherent to suppose that time should begin or end. Aristotle maintains that every change must take place within a longer time-scale than is occupied by the change itself.[8] This is becauses he regards time, space and change as all infinitely divisible, so that there is no least amount of any of them. It follows that any stretch of time or space in which a change occurs must contain a smaller stretch which ends earlier and starts later, and be contained in a larger stretch which ends later and starts earlier. Otherwise we would have the possibility of a period of time (or space) between the particular change and the adjacent states of affairs.

If time itself were to be created or destroyed, these would be events and, as such, governed by the general conceptual conditions for the temporal extent of changes. So the event of the creation of time would have to be preceded by some time, and the event of the destruction of time succeeded by some time; but this contradicts the very description of these particular events. So unless we reject the view that time is continuous, not composed of extended atoms, we must allow that time does not begin or end. There is an immediate consequence for the duration of change in general, since time is dependent on change. Time is what measures change; so where there is no change between two supposedly successive states of affairs, they are in fact identical. It follows that there is no beginning or end to change.[9]

We can take this a step further. Just as time depends on change, so change depends on substances which undergo it. In Chapter 5 we saw how Aristotle uses the analysis of change of substance to elucidate all other types of change.[10] This strategy was promised earlier, in Chapter 3, when we noted that the theory of categories could help to unravel the ambiguity in talk about change.[11] The theory explains how predicates of substance are primary among all predicates. Thus any change at all is reducible to a change involving a substance.

Therefore if change has no beginning or end, the substances presupposed by change are likewise without start or finish. The foregoing considerations provide an argumentative route taking us from the eternity of time to the eternity of substance. Here is the outcome: 'Substances are primary among things; and if all are perishable, everything is perishable. But it is impossible for change either to arise or to perish (since it always was), nor for time.'[12] But a familiar danger lurks in this way of formulating the important interim conclusion which Aristotle reaches here. He appears to infer that among substances there is at least one that is not perishable, while all that the premisses about time and change entail is that there should always be some substance or other. The stronger conclusion that the same one substance always exists does not seem to follow. So it is easy to fault this version of the cosmological argument for depending on the quantifier-shift fallacy; and, of course, this complaint is often made against other versions of the same argument.[13]

Aristotle's argument would be seriously damaged if this charge could be sustained. For as his argument moves on to its second stage, he will assume that what needs to be explained further is the existence of a single substance which undergoes eternal change. His account of the cause of eternal change proceeds on the assumption that one such cause will be sufficient to provide the explanation or, at least, that one among a plurality of causes will be primary. If the conclusion that there is at least one substance forever undergoing change is ill-founded, this weakness will infect all the further development of the argument.

Aristotle does indeed have a reply to this objection. The eternity of time is guaranteed by not just *any* change. He is looking for a mode of change which will support the uniformity and regularity of time. The question of uniformity is important because a change in the pace of time would require regular time to register it. This point is not verificationist: it is simply that there would be an intrinsic incoherence in the conception of time running at variable speed.[14]

Aristotle argues that only one kind of change can satisfy the conditions for the uniformity of time, and this is circular locomotion. Given his views about the spatial finitude of the universe and the fixity of natural kinds, all changes other than change of place and all rectilinear locomotion must begin and end; and his theory of dynamics states that the rate of change varies according to whether a change is near its beginning or its end.[15] So only locomotion in a circle can go on forever and thus maintain itself at a uniform rate. Does such a change actually occur? Aristotle can invoke the familiar empirical fact that the fixed stars exhibit this kind of motion; indeed they confirm his theoretical argument by serving as a measure of the rate of the sun's passage through the constellations—that is, as a measure of the year.[16] There is nothing inappropriate about using empirical considerations to clarify and support what is otherwise a largely theoretical investigation, since his whole argument is directed to the factual issue of the nature and ultimate cause of the universe around us.

So Aristotle does not merely assume that there is some one substance which always undergoes change; he provides independent support for this way of construing the thesis that some substance is always changing. We can now move to the second stage of the argument. The leading idea here is that self-motion, strictly interpreted, is impossible. The cause of change must be something different in kind from what it causes. Stage one of Aristotle's argument has some antecedents in Plato's speculations on cosmic motion; but in this second stage he diverges radically from Plato.

Aristotle's argument against self-motion has two versions. The first version uses the notion of potentiality. Real change, as opposed to replacement, requires potentiality; the potentiality remains constant, while it is actualised in various forms. The case which concerns us in the present argument is that of the sphere of the fixed stars. The actual spatial position of this varies constantly, but it is invariant in its potentiality for circular locomotion. So the movement of this object combines actuality and potentiality; and we need to consider further the relation between the two.

At first it may seem that potentiality is prior to actuality; for if something is actual, it is also possible, but the converse is not the case. In fact the priority is the other way round.[17] If a thing exists at all, it will actually be something or other; if in addition it has a potentiality, this will be a potentiality for it actually to be something or other. Actuality is logically prior to potentiality; we have seen this idea worked out in some detail in the conceptual argument for teleology.[18] The distinction between actuality and potentiality must be recognised as we analyse any movement, including the ultimate cosmic cause of movement.

This is why Plato's proposal that self-motion is the primary form of motion fails. A self-mover must combine actuality and potentiality; and if such a thing is primary, it will be quite impossible to distinguish the elements of actuality and potentiality within it. So the priority of actuality will have to be given up if we follow Plato's proposal. A self-mover will be an actually eternal substance; but at the same time it will have no more than the potentiality for eternity. Aristotle argues that this conception is self-contradictory.[19]

The second version of the argument against self-motion uses the contrast between matter and form. A substance has a potential for change if and only if it has matter. Conversely, something which lacks matter and exists only as form, will be wholly exempt from change. Now if we examine the idea of a substance which is the cause of its own change, we find that two factors must be distinguished. There is something which is constantly altering its condition as the change proceeds; this is the matter. There is also something which constantly gives structure and continuity to the change; this is the form. A self-moving substance, strictly understood, must be one in which matter and form are identical—an impossibility.[20]

This is not to deny that there may be a looser way of understanding self-change which is not open to these difficulties. Aristotle agrees that there is a perfectly obvious and acceptable distinction between things which can move themselves and those which cannot.[21] Roughly, living animals fall within the first kind and other substances within the second.[22] Whatever may emerge from a stricter inspection of the nature of change, this distinction must survive. But when we are testing the thesis that self-change is *primary*, the strict interpretation is necessary. A fine analysis may reveal a complexity in the self-moving substance, of such a kind that one part could cause another to change while itself remaining unchanged. He argues that in fact this is how it is with living animals. The animal's soul causes the movements of the body, while itself not undergoing movement; the body is the patient, not the agent of change.[23] A notable example of the application of this analysis is the human person.

When Aristotle declares self-motion to be impossible, sometimes he is speaking strictly, and sometimes less so. This does much to explain the different things that he says in different places on the cause of the motion of the fixed stars.[24] These variations have been taken as evidence of a development in his theory. When he speaks of the ultimate source of change as self-moving, Aristotle's position seems close to Plato's; but his rejection of this idea in other passages marks his distance from the Platonic view. This diagnosis of inconsistency and change of mind is wrong, as examination of the relation between the primary substance in motion and its cause will show. Meanwhile we shall not add obfuscation by confusing the strict and loose notions of self-change.

The Nature of God

We have reached the position that the ultimate cause of change in the universe is a substance which is itself exempt from change—an unmoved mover. It is without matter and purely actual; these attributes follow from its immutability. We have still to settle how such a substance can achieve the causal results which the argument has led us to expect of it. Given the natural presumption that anything which has any involvement in change is also liable to undergo change, this will not be straightforward. Aristotle finds this an attractive presumption. He refers to the causal inertness of mathematical entities and Platonic Forms in order to call their ontological status into question.[25] But he is able to deploy a crucial element in his own conception of causality to show how an unchanging cause of change can escape this objection. As he develops his defence, we begin to see that God is indeed the topic to which the whole argument is addressed.

The key causal idea is the final cause—the end-result for the sake of which something is done or happens. Where conscious deliberation is concerned, the final cause is the object of thought or desire; in a word, it is the good.[26] But, as we saw in the discussion of teleology, Aristotle recognises the operation of final causes far beyond the conscious sphere. A final cause need not itself be affected when it causes something else to change. Such causation provides a good illustration of the difference between 'Cambridge' and real change. When a thing becomes or ceases to be an object of thought or desire, this may not be due to any change in it; the change may reside entirely in the mind that thinks or desires it. This lesson will apply equally in cases where the change is unconscious; indeed it is even more plausible here. So if the ultimate cause of change is a final cause, it may itself remain unaffected by the movement which it produces.[27]

Aristotle has established that the unchanging substance causes movement 'like what is loved'.[28] At this point there appears to be a startling shift in the terms of the discussion. After talking about change and its ultimate cause, he now begins to speak of the ideal life and mental operation of a pure mind.[29] The subject becomes explicitly theological. How has this topic come out of the earlier cosmological argument? This is where the flamboyant idea of a mind which thinks about its own thought, enters the discussion. Although there is every reason to suppose that Aristotle took the idea fully seriously, some commentators have found it incomprehensible; and clearly it needs elucidation.[30] First we must understand how the transfer from the cosmological to the theological idiom occurs.

The main work is done by the thesis that the activity of thinking is identical with its content. We examined earlier what this thesis says in general about the nature of thought and how it is related to parallel analyses of perception and other faculties of the soul. In these more general accounts of the ways in which human beings interact with the world Aristotle has to qualify the identity thesis.[31] But the reasons which require this qualification in the general case, do not apply to the present topic of pure abstract thought. Here there is no way of distinguishing the mind from its object. Both lack matter, and so there is no possibility for the mind to do other than think its thought or for the object of thought to be other than thought.[32]

In the *De Philosophia* Aristotle presents an argument which moves from the perfection of God to his immutability. Any change in a perfect being must be for the worse.[33] This gives a foretaste of the medieval ontological argument for the existence of God; and Aristotle anticipates the later exercise even more closely when he adapts the *De Philosophia* argument to his investigation of pure mind in the *Metaphysics*. If a perfect mind were to think of something less than perfect, this would be incompatible with its perfection. But this mind and its thought is the greatest perfection. So the perfection about which the mind thinks is none other than itself.[34] The argument moves from the conception of a perfect being to its existence, in exactly the style of ontological arguments; to see this is to appreciate more fully the significance of the thesis that God thinks about his own thinking.

Aristotle is a monotheist. He argues for this in a section which some have wrongly taken to make difficulties for his main thesis about the first cause of change.[35] Recent work on astronomy had convinced Aristotle that the observed movements of heavenly bodies, especially the planets, must be explained by a plurality of causes. The problem was first raised by Plato, to calculate the smallest number of circular geocentric movements which would match the phenomena; and solutions were elaborated by Eudoxus and Callippus.[36] Aristotle discusses these proposals and advances one of his own; its mathematics are more applied than is the case with the other theorists. The mathematical details do not concern us, but we need to consider the implication of allowing that there is more than one unmoved mover. Aristotle maintains that just as the fixed stars must have their particular circular movement explained by a cause which is exempt from change, so this principle of explanation has to be extended to each of the physical movements which contribute to the phenomena; each is caused by its particular unmoved mover.[37]

Each unmoved mover is an immaterial, purely actual substance. This raises the question of how a number of such substances can be differentiated. As Aristotle points out, things which are of the same essential kind can differ only by virtue of their matter; yet unmoved movers lack matter.[38] The answer is that this difficulty depends on an elliptical characterisation of each unmoved mover. The movers are ordered in a series, so that there is a first, a second and so on; and we saw in Chapter 7 that Aristotle believes it erroneous to abstract from the members of a series the general principle of their ordering.[39] So there is no need to invoke matter to account for the difference between the first unmoved mover and the second unmoved mover, and similarly for all the others, since these differences are adequately secured by the formal aspect of their nature.

What would be impossible would be more than one *first* unmoved mover. This is the very impossibility to which Aristotle adverts in this argument. There cannot be more than one universe, since each would require a first unmoved mover and a plurality of *these* is incoherent. A universe is an ordered whole. It can be plural, but its many parts must connect to form a single system.[40] Aristotle is aware that the introduction of a plurality of unmoved movers may open the way for misunderstanding, or even criticism, on the ground that it infringes the unity of the universe. By way of response he provides an argument for the thesis that there can be only one universe. While the main considerations deployed here are cosmological, the theological dimension of this argument for monotheism should also be recognised.

We have considered one alleged incoherence in Aristotle's argument and have found that it does not stand scrutiny. The second major problem concerns the relation between an astronomical movement and its unmoved mover. The difficulty is highlighted by the plurality of unmoved movers, but it would still arise even if their number were limited to one. For each celestial body moving in its eternal circular motion around the earth we have an unmoved mover which causes its motion finally, somewhat in the manner of an object of thought or desire. It seems that Aristotle's account should explicitly mention a further factor on which it is in fact silent; the celestial bodies must have minds if they are to be motivated by their causes.[41] His scheme is apparently committed to a trio of entities—the celestial body, its mind, and the unmoved mover—or rather to as many trios as there are distinct celestial motions. If he were to deny the need for the celestial mind, there would be no satisfactory account of the causal relation between the two items. It has been argued that in other works, most notably the *De Caelo*, Aristotle recognises that the celestial bodies have minds;[42] and the separation of thought from the astronomical body has been taken to be a development in the *Physics* and *Metaphysics* from that earlier position. Whether or not the developmental theory carries conviction, the *Metaphysics* account seems to lack an important element which Aristotle mentions elsewhere.

But these criticisms are also based on a mistake. There is a compelling reason why there is no room for a celestial mind beside the unmoved mover. The point is clearly made in the main argument in the *Metaphysics* that a purely actual object of thought can be grasped only by a purely actual mind; it is a general condition of such actualities that each member of the pair is identical with the other. The celestial mind, which is said to be underplayed in Aristotle's account, would have to be indistinguishable from the mind of the unmoved mover if it were engaged in thinking the primary object of thought; it would, moreover, be indistinguishable from the ultimate cause, since it would be identical with it by virtue of actually thinking it. On both counts, then, the celestial mind cannot occupy a position extra to and distinct from that of the unmoved mover.

How can the unmoved mover be a final cause to the astronomical body? The answer, I suggest, is as soul to body.

In his general analysis in the *De Anima* of the relation between soul and body, Aristotle argues that the soul is the final cause of a living animal body, mainly on the ground that the exercise of life faculties is what gives purpose and point to the bodily constitution of the animal.[43] Nobody supposes that this conception is incoherent because it requires that the body must have some conscious aim to possess psychic status. The kind of teleology invoked here is the unconscious variety which figures so widely in Aristotle's work on causality; the bodily constitution is explained in terms of the function which it performs.

A celestial body has but one function, that of sustaining eternal circular movement. So the soul which is its final cause can be equally simple in nature. In view of the theoretical perfection of this body, it is appropriate that the kind of soul for whose sake it moves should be a pure mind. The rationale is that as the movement of the heavenly bodies is the mathematically ideal motion, the life which it promotes is essentially intelligent.[44] In terms of our experience of more familiar life forms, there is a particular kind of soul which corresponds to this kind of life; and this is the mind.

Suppose that the astronomical body and the unmoved mover which causes its motion, are related as body and soul. This will explain why in some contexts Aristotle appears to regard a self-moving substance as the primary cosmic factor. This is a correct account of the movement if it is viewed grossly; in the same sense animals are self-moving by contrast with non-animals. But on fine inspection it turns out to be false, since we must distinguish a soul and a body.[45]

There is one text which appears hard to reconcile with this interpretation. In the *Physics* Aristotle says that the unmoved mover is 'not even accidentally moved';[46] yet a human or animal soul is moved accidentally, by virtue of the movement of the body which it informs.[47] Since the cosmic body is similarly in movement, how can the cosmic soul fail to be moved accidentally? If it cannot, must we not reject the idea that the soul/body relation is the correct one to apply to the cosmic case?

On reflection this objection becomes hard to sustain. The celestial bodies are spherical bands revolving uniformly about a central point. Taken as a whole, they do not change position;

by contrast, the bodies of animals change their entire location. We can make good sense of the statement that the souls of animals are moved along with their bodies. But there is no parallel reason to say the same of the unmoved mover of the sphere of the fixed stars.

Aristotle's philosophical argument for the existence of God is now complete. It is a *tour de force*, grand in scale and highly technical in detail. For much of the time he relies on claims that are much more thoroughly investigated in other contexts. But he applies them to the present topic in a careful way; and his account can be defended against the charges of confusion and omission which have been brought against it. The main elements in the earlier part of the argument belong to cosmology; but with the introduction of some key theses from psychology the argument works to a theologically significant conclusion.

Theology

How convincing is the theology? The conception of God contemplating nothing but his own contemplation has struck many as profoundly unsatisfactory. For those whose views of God are shaped in the Judaeo-Christian tradition, the idea of a God whose perfection derives from his lack of concern for human affairs, seems strange indeed.

The strangeness was apparent to the Greeks too. Plato in the *Parmenides* examines the consequences for his theory of Forms if the distinctness of the perfect realm of Forms from the imperfect realm of particulars is strongly emphasised.[48] If there is a sharp distinction between the realms, it is plausible that where one item is related to another, each of them will belong to the same realm. But this produces serious difficulty for the related items of knowledge and reality. Our knowledge, being particular and imperfect, must be of imperfect and particular reality—the world of physical, perceptible objects which surrounds us; so we cannot have knowledge of the Forms. This difficulty has been much discussed, and it certainly impressed Aristotle as revealing a deep problem in the theory of Forms.[49]

The other side of the problem has received less comment; and yet it is very pertinent to Aristotle's theology. A consequence of the sharp separation of Forms and particulars is that perfect knowledge must have perfect reality as its object; whatever is known to God, who has perfect knowledge, is nothing other than the Forms. So God's knowledge does not extend to the other realm, the world which comprises us humans and our surroundings.[50]

In the *Parmenides* this second part of the problem is regarded as even more shocking than the first; and in reacting this way Plato not only agrees with the literary culture of Greece, he also represents the predominant attitude among philosophers who were seriously interested in religion.[51] A comparison of the views of the Stoics and the Epicureans (even though they came later than Plato and Aristotle) can cast light on this. The Stoics make extensive use of the concept of God in their philosophy. For them a major problem is to explain how God's concern for the affairs of the world can be reconciled with a deterministic view of natural processes. So they write essays on God's providence, and they take seriously the issues in the philosophy of space and time which must arise on an interactionist conception of God's relation to the natural world.[52]

Contrast the Epicureans. They acknowledge religion as a psychological phenomenon; their empiricism does not allow them to deny the truth of claims to have direct experience of God. But they theorise that God (or the Gods) thus authenticated has no further causal role in the universe, except as part of the pathology of human wretchedness. Properly conceived, the divine nature is independent of human concerns. So the theism of the Epicureans discounts as diseased any awareness of the role that God has in the regulation of mundane or human affairs.[53]

Aristotle's position in this debate is distinctive and interesting. He accepts the conclusion of the second part of the argument in the *Parmenides*: God has no concern for human affairs. Unlike Plato, and unlike the Stoics, he finds no problem in this conclusion. But he would not accept the Epicurean interpretation of God as irrelevant to the good ordering of the world around us. The final part of what he says about God in the *Metaphysics* will reveal how his conception of sound theological analysis is based on respect for popular insight.

An adequate account of the nature of God and his relation to the world must explain the goodness of things. Is value derived from some particular source, or does it reside in the world as a whole? Aristotle argues that this choice between transcendent and immanent conceptions is an avoidable dichotomy. He compares the case of an army. An army is good provided that it has both a good general and a good organisation under him.[54] The comparison can mislead. Is the general not concerned with his officers and troops, and does this not produce a fundamental disanalogy with God in his unconcern for anything but his own thought? This is to mistake the proper activity of the general. It is true that the general is not concerned only with himself, and to this extent there is indeed some disanalogy with God. But it is wrong to see the general's attention as properly directed to his subordinates; instead, his attention should be focused on the enemy and the task of winning the war. It is for his troops to pay attention to him, not vice versa; and if he focuses his attention in the right way, this excellence will be extended to the rest of the army.

The value of the army is located in a particular, transcendent source and also is immanent in the whole army. In the same way the goodness of the universe resides both in the pure thought of a God who is beyond matter and change, and in the whole collection of material and mutable things in their causal dependence on this God. The perfection of the self-absorption of the primary substance makes all other things in the universe better than they otherwise would be.

This account of the goodness of things well illustrates the formula which Aristotle uses to describe the place of theology among the other sciences—'universal inasmuch as it is primary'. His work is a notable contribution to the philosophy of religion. It crowns an edifice of theoretical studies as it draws on his investigations of substance, change and mind. The discussion of God combines technical and popular elements in a way that marks it as a quintessentially Aristotelian product.

Notes

1 *Top.* A11, 105a5-6; *Cael.* A3, 270b5-6; *Met.* Λ8, 1074b3-10.

2 Berkeley, *Three Dialogues between Hylas and Philonous* II 212-15;

Descartes, *Fifth Meditation*, pp.184-5, in E.S. Haldane and G.R.T. Ross (eds.), *The Philosophical Works of Descartes*, vol.1 (Cambridge, 1911).

3 *Met.* E1, 1026a30-1.

4 *Top.* A1, 100b21-3; A14, 105a34-b1.

5 This issue is well explored by J.C.A. Gaskin, *The Quest for Eternity* (Penguin, 1984), pp.25-36.

6 W. Jaeger, *Aristotle*, transl. R. Robinson (Oxford, 1948), pp.342-67. W.K.C. Guthrie, 'The Development of Aristotle's Theology', *Classical Quarterly* 27 (1933), 162-71 and 28 (1934), 90-8 offers a rather different, although still developmental, account.

7 Plato *Phaedrus* 245d; *Laws* 894e-5b.

8 *Met.* Λ6, 1071b7-9; *Phys.* Z5, 236a35-b18. See further, R.R.K. Sorabji, 'Aristotle on the Instant of Change', *Aristotelian Society Supplementary Volume* 50 (1976), 69-89.

9 *Met.* Λ6, 1071b9-10; *Phys.* Δ11, 219a33-b5; *Phys.* Θ1, 251b10-2a5.

10 *Met.* Λ6, 1071b4-7; Chapter 5, pp.86-9 above.

11 Chapter 3, pp.53-4 above.

12 *Met.* Λ6, 1071b5-7.

13 G.E.M. Anscombe and P.T. Geach, *Three Philosophers* (Blackwell, 1961), p.60; A.J.P. Kenny, *The Five Ways* (London, 1969), pp.56-7, 64-7.

14 *Met.* Λ6, 1072a9-18; cf. *Phys.* Θ7, 260a21-b7; Δ10, 218b3-18.

15 *Cael.* A8, 277a27-b8; *Phys.* Θ9, 265b11-16; cf. *G.C.* B11, 338b6-19.

16 *Met.* Z16, 1040b27-1a3; *Met.* Λ5, 1071a15-16; Λ6, 1072a17-18.

17 *Met.* Λ6, 1071b12-26.

18 *Met.* Θ8, 1049b12-17; see Chapter 5, pp.97-8 above.

19 *Met.* Λ6, 1071b17-20; *Phys.* Θ5, 257b2-12; *Met.* Θ8, 1049b19-25.

20 *Met.* Λ6, 1071b20-2; Λ7, 1072b4-8.

21 *Phys.* Θ4, 254b12-18; B1, 192b27-33.

22 *Cael.* B2, 284b15-34.

23 *Phys.* Θ4, 255a15-18; *De An.* A3, 406a1-10.

24 *Cael.* A9, 279a23-b3, and B3, 286a9-12 attribute self-motion to the first cause, while *Cael.* B6, 288a27-b7, and Δ3, 311a9-12 seem to deny this.

25 *Met.* Λ10, 1075b27-37; A9, 991b3-9.

26 *Met.* Λ7, 1072a26-b3; cf. A3, 983a31-2.

27 For Aristotle's concern for reciprocal causation between agent and patient, cf. *G.C.* A7, 324a24-b13; *G.A.* Δ3, 768b16-25.

28 *Met.* Λ7, 1072b3.

29 *Met.* Λ7, 1072b13-15.

30 *Met.* Λ7, 1072b19-21; Λ9, 1074b33-5. This is the plain meaning of Aristotle's words, but some have tried to interpret them differently: G.E.M. Anscombe and P.T. Geach, *Three Philosophers* (Blackwell, 1961), pp.59-60; R. Norman, 'Aristotle's philosopher-God', *Phronesis* 14 (1969), 63-74.

31 See Chapter 7, pp.128-31 above.

32 *Met.* Λ7, 1072b26-30; Λ9, 1075a3-5.

33 *De Philosophia* fr.16.

34 *Met.* Λ9, 1074b25-33.

35 e.g. Jaeger, *Aristotle* (see n.6 above), pp.346-54. For a much sounder

view of this passage, see P. Merlan, 'Aristotle's Unmoved Movers', *Traditio* 4 (1946), 1-30.

36 See D.R. Dicks, *Early Greek Astronomy to Aristotle* (Thames & Hudson, 1970), pp.108, 190.

37 *Met*. Λ8, 1073a26-b1, 1074a14-16.

38 *Met*. Λ8, 1074a33-6; Z8, 1034a5-8; cf. *Cael*. A9, 278a15-20.

39 *Met*. Λ8, 1073b1-3; Chapter 7, pp.123-5 above.

40 In the argument for the uniqueness of the universe at *Met*. Λ8, 1074a31-8, there is emphasis on the *primacy* of the first unmoved mover. For the theological significance of unity in the universe, see *Met*. Λ10, 1075a23-5, 1075b37-6a4.

41 W.D. Ross, *Aristotle's Metaphysics* vol.1 (Oxford, 1924), pp.cxxxvi-cxl, spells out the complicated scheme of entities to which he thinks Aristotle committed; but he quite misleadingly suggests that all of these are actually mentioned, and so he fails to consider the significance of Aristotle's silences.

42 W.K.C. Guthrie, *Aristotle On the Heavens* (Harvard, 1939), pp.xxix-xxxvi.

43 *De An*. B4, 415b15-20; *P.A*. A1, 641a27-8.

44 *Met*. Λ7, 1072b4-10; cf. *Cael*. A2, 269a18-b2.

45 See D.J. Furley, 'Self-Movers', in A.O. Rorty (ed.), *Essays on Aristotle's Ethics* (California, 1980), pp.55-67.

46 *Phys*. Θ6, 259b20-31.

47 *De An*. A3, 406a5-7, b7-15.

48 Plato *Parmenides* 133b-4e.

49 Cf. *Top*. Z8, 146b36-7a10; see my *Aristotle's Concept of Dialectic* (Cambridge, 1977), pp.94-8.

50 *Parmenides* 134c4-e8.

51 W.K.C. Guthrie, *The Greeks and their Gods* (London, 1950), pp.364-7.

52 See S. Sambursky, *Physics of the Stoics* (London, 1959), pp.65-6.

53 J.M. Rist, *Epicurus: An Introduction* (Cambridge, 1972), pp.146-8, 161-2.

54 *Met*. Λ10, 1075a11-15.

Bibliography

The main purpose of this bibliography is to list the works cited in the text. I do not attempt a full bibliography of modern work on Aristotle. I have, however, included some publications, not mentioned in the text, which have influenced its argument.

A recent bibliography of work on Aristotle is:

J. Barnes, M. Schofield and R. Sorabji, (eds.), *Aristotle: A Bibliography* (Oxford, 1977).

The best way to keep abreast of ongoing publication is through the relevant sections of the two bibliographical Journals:

Répertoire Bibliographique de la Philosophie (Louvain). *L'Année Philologique* (Paris).

Ackrill, J. L., *Aristotle's Categories and De Interpretatione* (Oxford, 1963).

Ackrill, J. L., *Aristotle the Philosopher* (Oxford, 1981).

Anscombe, G. E. M., 'Thought and Action in Aristotle', in R. Bambrough (ed.), *New Essays on Plato and Aristotle* (London, 1965), pp. 143-58.

Anscombe, G. E. M., 'Aristotle and the Sea Battle', in J. M. E. Moravcsik (ed.), *Aristotle: A Collection of Critical Essays* (New York, 1967), pp. 15-33.

Anscombe, G. E. M., 'Causality and Extensionality', in *Collected Papers*, vol. 2 (Oxford, 1981), pp. 173-9.

Anscombe, G. E. M. and Geach, P. T., *Three Philosophers* (Blackwell, 1961).

Ayer, A. J., *The Problem of Knowledge* (London, 1956).

Bambrough, R., 'Aristotle on Justice: A Paradigm of Philosophy', in R. Bambrough (ed.), *New Essays on Plato and Aristotle* (London, 1965), pp. 159-74.

Barker, E., *Greek Political Theory* (London, 1960).

Barnes, J., 'Aristotle's Theory of Demonstration', *Phronesis* 14 (1969), 123-52.
Barnes, J., 'Aristotle's Concept of Mind', *Proceedings of the Aristotelian Society* 72 (1971–72), 101-14.
Barnes, J., Introduction to *Aristotle's Ethics* (Penguin, 1976).
Barnes, J., *Aristotle* (Oxford, 1982).
Bennett, J., *Kant's Analytic* (Cambridge, 1966).
Berkeley, G., *Philosophical Works*, ed. M. R. Ayers (Dent, 1975).
Burnyeat, M., (ed.), *Notes on Aristotle's Metaphysics Zeta* (Oxford, 1979).
Charles, D., *Aristotle's Philosophy of Action* (London, 1984).
Charlton, W., *Aristotle's Physics I, II* (Oxford, 1970).
Cherniss, H., *The Riddle of the Early Academy* (New York, 1962).
Clark, S. R. L., *Aristotle's Man* (Oxford, 1975).
Cooper, J. M., 'Aristotle on Friendship' in A. O. Rorty (ed.), *Essays on Aristotle's Ethics* (California, 1980), pp. 301-40.
Crombie, I. M., *An Examination of Plato's Doctrines*, vol. 2 (London, 1963).
Crossman, R. H. S., *Plato Today* (London, 1937).
Davidson, D., *Essays on Actions and Events* (Oxford, 1980).
Davidson, D., *Inquiries into Truth and Interpretation* (Oxford, 1984).
Dennett, D. C., *Brainstorms* (Harvester, 1978).
Descartes, *Meditations*, in E. S. Haldane and G. R. T. Ross (eds.), *The Philosophical Works of Descartes*, vol. 1 (Cambridge, 1911).
Dicks, D. R., *Early Greek Astronomy to Aristotle* (Thames & Hudson, 1970).
Dummett, M. A. E., 'Can an Effect Precede its Cause?', in *Truth and Other Enigmas* (London, 1978), pp. 319-32.
Dummett, M. A. E., 'Can analytical philosophy be systematic, and ought it to be?', in *Truth and Other Enigmas* (London, 1978), pp. 437-58.
Dummett, M. A. E., *Frege: Philosophy of Language* (London, 1981).
Evans, J. D. G., 'Aristotle on Relativism' *Philosophical Quarterly* 24 (1974), 193-203.
Evans, J. D. G., *Aristotle's Concept of Dialectic* (Cambridge, 1977).
Evans, J. D. G., 'Berkeley on Conceiving the Unconceived', *Irish Philosophcal Journal* 2 (1985), 79-93.
Finley, M. I., *Ancient Slavery and Modern Ideology* (London, 1980).
Follesdal, D., 'Quantification into Causal Contexts', in L. Linsky (ed.), *Reference and Modality* (Oxford, 1971), pp. 52-62.
Fortenbaugh, W., 'Aristotle's Rhetoric on Emotions', *Archiv für Geschichte der Philosophie* 52 (1970), 40-70.
Frede, M., 'Categories in Aristotle', in D. J. O'Meara (ed.), *Studies in Aristotle* (Washington, 1981), pp. 1-24.

Furley, D. J., 'Self-Movers', in A. O. Rorty (ed.), *Essays on Aristotle's Ethics* (California, 1980), pp. 55-67.

Gaskin, J. C. A., *The Quest for Eternity* (Penguin, 1984).

Geach, P. T., 'Good and Evil', in P. Foot (ed.), *Theories of Ethics* (Oxford, 1967), pp. 64-73.

Geach, P. T., 'God's Relation to the World', in *Logic Matters* (Blackwell, 1972), pp. 318-27.

Geach, P. T. and Black, M. (eds.), *The Philosophical Writings of Gottlob Frege* (Blackwell, 1960).

Goodman, N., *Fact, Fiction, and Forecast* (London, 1954).

Grene, M., *A Portrait of Aristotle* (London, 1963).

Guthrie, W. K. C., *Aristotle On the Heavens* (Harvard, 1939).

Guthrie, W. K. C., 'The Development of Aristotle's Theology', *Classical Quarterly* 27 (1933), 162-71, and 28 (1934), 90-8.

Guthrie, W. K. C., *The Greeks and their Gods* (London, 1950).

Guthrie, W. K. C., *A History of Greek Philosophy*, vols. 1–2 (Cambridge, 1962–65).

Hamlyn, D. W., *Aristotle's 'De Anima', Books II and III* (Oxford, 1968).

Hardie, W. F. R., *Aristotle's Ethical Theory* (Oxford, 1968).

Hare, R. M., 'Geach: Good and Evil', in P. Foot (ed.), *Theories of Ethics* (Oxford, 1967), pp. 74-82.

Hart, W. D., 'The Epistemology of Abstract Objects', *Aristotelian Society Supplementary Volume* 53 (1979), 153-65.

Hicks, R. D., *Aristotle De Anima* (Cambridge, 1907).

Huby, P., 'The First Discovery of the Freewill Problem', *Philosophy* 42 (1967), 353-62.

Hursthouse, R., 'A False Doctrine of the Mean', *Proceedings of the Aristotelian Society* 81 (1980–81), 57-72.

Irwin, T. H., *Plato's Moral Theory* (Oxford, 1977).

Irwin, T. H., 'The Metaphysical and Psychological Basis of Aristotle's Ethics', in A. O. Rorty (ed.), *Essays on Aristotle's Ethics* (California, 1980), pp. 35-53.

Jaeger, W., *Aristotle*, transl. R. Robinson (Oxford, 1948).

Kant, I., *Critique of Pure Reason*, transl. N. Kemp Smith (Macmillan, 1933).

Kenny, A. J. P., 'The Practical Syllogism and Incontinence', *Phronesis* 11 (1966), 163-84.

Kenny, A. J. P., *The Five Ways* (London, 1969).

Kenny, A. J. P., *The Aristotelian Ethics* (Oxford, 1978).

Kirk, G. S., Raven, J. E. and Schofield, M., (eds.), *The Presocratic Philosophers* (Cambridge, 1983).

Kirwan, C., *Aristotle's Metaphysics Books* Γ, Δ, E (Oxford, 1971).

Kripke, S., 'Naming and Necessity', in D. Davidson and G. Harman (eds.), *Semantics of Natural Language* (Dordrecht, 1972), pp. 253-355.

Kripke, S., *Wittgenstein on Rules and Private Language* (Blackwell, 1982).
Lemmon, E. J., 'Moral Dilemmas', *Philosophical Review* 71 (1962), 139-58.
Leyden, W. von, *Aristotle on Equality and Justice* (Macmillan, 1985).
Lloyd, G. E. R., *Aristotle: The Growth and Structure of his Thought* (Cambridge, 1968).
Lloyd-Jones, H., *The Justice of Zeus* (California, 1971).
Locke, J., *An Essay Concerning Human Understanding*, ed. A. D. Woozley (Collins, 1964).
Lukasiewicz, J., *Aristotle's Syllogistic from the Standpoint of Modern Formal Logic* (Oxford, 1957).
McDowell, J., 'Are Moral Requirements Hypothetical Imperatives?', *Aristotelian Society Supplementary Volume* 52 (1978), 13-29.
McGinn, C., 'Mental States, Natural Kinds and Psychophysical Laws', *Aristotelian Society Supplementary Volume* 52 (1978), 195-220.
McGinn, C., *The Character of Mind* (Oxford, 1982).
Mackie, J. L., *The Cement of the Universe* (Oxford, 1974).
Mackie, J. L., *Ethics* (Penguin, 1977).
Macleod, C. W., 'Thucydides on Faction (3.82-83)', *Proceedings of the Cambridge Philological Society* NS 25 (1979), 52-68.
Marras, A., 'Scholastic Roots of Brentano's Concept of Intentionality', in L. McAlister (ed.), *The Philosophy of Brentano* (London, 1976), pp. 128-39.
Matson, W. I., 'Why isn't the mind–body problem ancient?', in P. K. Feyerabend and G. Maxwell (eds.), *Mind, Matter, and Method* (Minneapolis, 1966), pp. 92-102.
Merlan, P., 'Aristotle's Unmoved Movers', *Traditio* 4 (1946), 1-30.
Moore, G. E., *Principia Ethica* (Cambridge, 1903).
Moraux, P., 'La méthode d'Aristote dans l'étude du ciel', in S. Mansion (ed.), *Aristote et les Problèmes de Méthode* (Louvain, 1961), pp. 173-94.
Mulgan, R. G., *Aristotle's Political Theory* (Oxford, 1977).
Nagel, T., 'Subjective and Objective', in *Mortal Questions* (Cambridge, 1979), pp. 196-213.
Norman, R., 'Aristotle's philosopher-God', *Phronesis* 14 (1969), 63-74.
Nowell-Smith, P. H., *Ethics* (London, 1954).
Owen, G. E. L., 'Logic and metaphysics in some earlier works of Aristotle', in I. Düring and G. E. L. Owen (eds.), *Aristotle and Plato in the Mid-Fourth Century* (Göteborg, 1960), pp. 163-90.
Owen, G. E. L., 'A Proof in the *Peri Ideon*', in R. E. Allen (ed.), *Studies in Plato's Metaphysics* (London, 1965), pp. 293-312.
Owen, G. E. L., 'Aristotle on the Snares of Ontology', in R. Bambrough (ed.), *New Essays on Plato and Aristotle* (London,

1965), pp. 69-95.

Owen, G. E. L., 'The Platonism of Aristotle', *Proceedings of the British Academy* 51 (1965), 125-50.

Owen, G. E. L., 'Dialectic and Eristic in the Treatment of the Forms', in G. E. L. Owen (ed.), *Aristotle on Dialectic* (Oxford, 1968), pp. 103-25.

Owen, G. E. L., 'Particular and General', *Proceedings of the Aristotelian Society* 79 (1978–79), 1-21.

Phillips, D. Z., 'In Search of the Moral "Must": Mrs Foot's Fugitive Thought', *Philosophical Quarterly* 27 (1977), 140-57.

Plato, *Opera*, 5 vols., ed. J. Burnet (Oxford, 1901–7).

Popper, K. R., *The Open Society and its Enemies*, vol.1 (London, 1945).

Quine, W. V., 'Two Dogmas of Empiricism', in *From a Logical Point of View* (New York, 1953), pp. 20-46.

Rist, J. M., *Epicurus: An Introduction* (Cambridge, 1972).

Robinson, H. M., 'Prime Matter in Aristotle', *Phronesis* 19 (1974), 168-88.

Ross, W. D., *Aristotle's Metaphysics*, vol.1 (Oxford, 1924).

Russell, B., *The Problems of Philosophy* (Oxford, 1967).

Ryle, G., *The Concept of Mind* (London, 1949).

Ryle, G., 'Letters and Syllables in Plato', *Philosophical Review* 69 (1960), 431-51.

Ryle, G., 'Categories', in *Collected Papers*, vol.2 (London, 1971) pp. 170-84.

Sambursky, S., *Physics of the Stoics* (London, 1959).

Santas, G., 'Aristotle on Practical Inference, the Explanation of Action and Akrasia', *Phronesis* 14 (1969), 162-89.

Schofield, M., '*Metaph.* Z3: some suggestions', *Phronesis* 17 (1972), 97-101.

Shiner, R., 'Ethical Perception in Aristotle', *Apeiron* 13 (1979), 79-85.

Sorabji, R. R. K., 'Body and Soul in Aristotle', *Philosophy* 49 (1974), 63-89.

Sorabji, R. R. K., 'Aristotle on the Instant of Change', *Aristotelian Society Supplementary Volume* 50 (1976), 69-89.

Sorabji, R. R. K., *Necessity, Cause and Blame* (London, 1980).

Strang, C., 'The Physical Theory of Anaxagoras', *Archiv für Geschichte der Philosophie* 45 (1963), 101-18.

Sykes, R. D., 'Form in Aristotle: Universal or Particular?', *Philosophy* 50 (1975), 311-31.

Urmson, J. O., 'Aristotle's Doctrine of the Mean', *American Philosophical Quarterly* 10 (1973), 223-30.

Waterlow, S., *Nature, Change, and Agency in Aristotle's Physics* (Oxford, 1982).

Waterlow, S., *Passage and Possibility* (Oxford, 1982).

White, N. P., 'Goodness and Human Aims in Aristotle's Ethics', in D. J. O'Meara (ed.), *Studies in Aristotle* (Washington, 1981), pp. 225-46.

Wiggins, D., 'Weakness of Will, Commensurability, and the Objects of Deliberation and Desire', *Proceedings of the Aristotelian Society* 79 (1978–79), 251-77.

Wilkes, K. V., *Physicalism* (London, 1978).

Williams, B. A. O., 'Egoism and Altruism', in *Problems of the Self* (Cambridge, 1973), pp. 250-65.

Woods, M. J., 'Problems in Metaphysics Z, Chapter 13', in J. M. E. Moravcsik (ed.), *Aristotle: A Collection of Critical Essays* (New York, 1967), pp. 215-38.

Wright, C. M. G., *Frege's Conception of Numbers as Objects* (Aberdeen, 1983).

General Index

Index of Passages

Aristotle

Plato